CHECK YOUR VOCABULARY FOR ENGLISH FOR THE

PET

A BLOOMSBURY REFERENCE BOOK

First published in Great Britain 2003

Bloomsbury Publishing Plc
38 Soho Square, London, W1D 3HB

© Bloomsbury Plc 2003
British Library Cataloguing in Publication Data
A catalogue entry for this book is available from the British Library
ISBN: 0-7475-6627-5

Typesetting and design by The Studio Publishing Services Ltd, Exeter
Printed in Italy by Legoprint

Contents

© Bloomsbury Publishing 2003. For reference see *Basic English Dictionary* (1-901659-96-8)

About this workbook

This workbook is designed to help you to use your English dictionary more efficiently, both in the classroom and the home. It is suitable for use with dictionaries at a lower-intermediate level such as the *English Study Dictionary* (ISBN: 1-901659-64-X, published by Bloomsbury Publishing) and *Basic English Dictionary* for Elementary and pre-Intermediate Students (ISBN: 1-901659-63-1, Bloomsbury Publishing). It will also help you to develop and practise the vocabulary you need to pass any lower-intermediate level examination such as the Cambridge revised PET (Preliminary English Test). The updated PET examination will be first administered in March 2004.

There are a variety of vocabulary exercises and activities that will help you to learn to recognise how words and expressions are presented in the *English Study* and *Basic English* Dictionaries, what they mean in different contexts, how to find other forms of the same word, and how they are pronounced. There are real-life tasks and exercises designed to help you to learn how to use English in order to communicate in everyday situations. These focus on the topics found in the revised PET examination.

The workbook is divided into seven sections.

Section 1.

Introduction. This section shows you how to use this book in the best possible way in order to learn the vocabulary you need for the Cambridge revised PET examination. It also shows you the different features of the dictionary and what they mean. It is a good idea to do the tasks in this section before you do anything else in this workbook.

Section 2.

Words & grammar. These units show you how word forms can have a different meaning or a different grammatical function and how you can use them for effective communication.

Section 3.

Verbs. These are units about the basic verbs and verb patterns you need to use in everyday situations.

Section 4.

Topics. These are theme-based units that help you to develop your vocabulary of everyday topics and areas like the ones you need to pass the Cambridge PET or other similar examinations.

Section 5.

Pronunciation & spelling. This section will show you how phonetic symbols can help you to understand the pronunciation of words, how stress can change the meaning of a word and how to spell and punctuate correctly.

Section 6.

Record sheets. These are photocopiable sheets on which you can record word forms, vocabulary items and useful verbs. You should keep these in your files for future reference, or for when you need to revise language points for the PET exam.

Section 7.

Answer key. The answer key is for you to check your answers after you have done them. Do not look at the answers until you have tried to do the exercises using your dictionary.

Glossary

The following abbreviations and words are used in this book and in your dictionary. Refer to these pages if you come across these words and are not sure what they mean.

adj. = adjective: It usually describes a noun
e.g. a <u>big</u>, <u>black</u> spider on the wall

adv. = adverb: It modifies a verb, an adjective, another adverb or a whole sentence
e.g. walk <u>slowly</u>, the snow was <u>very</u> thick

auxiliary verb: It forms part of a verb phrase
e.g. I <u>have</u> just seen John. He <u>was</u> eating lunch. <u>Did</u> you talk to him?

comparatives: Adjective or adverb forms that show comparison between two things
e.g. He is <u>shorter</u> than his brother, The weather is <u>better</u> today than it was yesterday

compound words: Adjectives or nouns made up of more than one word
e.g. a <u>five-star</u> hotel, under the <u>moonlight</u>

conjunction: A word that links different sections of a sentence
e.g. <u>Although</u> he left early, he was late and missed his train.

countable noun: It can have both singular and plural forms
e.g. dog / dogs, man / men.

irregular verb: It does not end with -ed in its past simple or past participle forms
e.g. eat – ate – eaten, swim – swam – swum

modal verb: It is used with another verb to show permission, intention, duty, etc.
e.g. <u>Can</u> I use the library? You <u>should</u> tidy your desk.

phrasal verb: A verb followed by a preposition which changes the main meaning of the verb
e.g. John <u>takes after</u> his brother.

pl. = plural: A word form used to show more than one person or thing
e.g. pens, they, people

prefix: Part of a word added to the beginning of a word to form a new word
e.g. <u>dis</u>appear, <u>mis</u>understand, <u>re</u>organise

pronoun: A word used instead of a noun,
e.g. me, he, it, they

superlatives: Adjective or adverb forms which show that someone or something has more of a certain quality than anyone or anything else
e.g. the <u>fastest</u> car, the <u>most difficult</u> task

suffix: Part of a word added to the end of a word to form another word
e.g. care<u>ful</u>, hope<u>less</u>, discuss<u>ion</u>

uncountable noun: A noun which does not have a plural form
e.g. homework, rice, cream

US = US or American English: A word or expression used in American English
e.g. color, highway, cookies

v. = verb: A word which shows an action, state or feeling
e.g. She <u>felt</u> very angry. He <u>lost</u> his wallet.

About PET

About PET

Check your Vocabulary for the PET Examination is designed to help candidates preparing for PET and will also give to all English-language learners the opportunity to practise and develop their vocabulary at this level. It covers most of the main topics and vocabulary areas examined by the PET examination. This workbook has been written according to the new specifications of PET as it has been recently reviewed (first administration of reviewed exam as of March 2004) and is up to date and in line with learners' needs around the world.

PET is provided by University of Cambridge ESOL (English for Speakers of Other Languages Examinations), a department of the University of Cambridge in England. PET is part of the Main Suite of Cambridge English examinations, which is closely linked to the Council of Europe's Common European Framework for modern languages (CEF).

The Preliminary English Test (PET) tests learners' competence in all language skills - Listening, Speaking, Reading and Writing - as well as assessing grammar and vocabulary with material from real-life situations, at a level approximately two thirds of the way towards FCE. It is the second level in the Cambridge ESOL five-level series of examinations - level B1 of the Common European Framework. PET recognises the ability to cope with everyday written and spoken communications and therefore provides evidence of practical skills. It indicates a candidate has sufficient ability to be of practical use in clerical, secretarial and managerial jobs, and in many industries such as tourism where contact with English speakers is required.

Studying for PET is a popular way to improve your language skills and use them in a wide range of contexts. PET is recognised by many employers and educational institutions as proof of intermediate-level English skills. Candidates who pass PET are expected to be at the Council of Europe Threshold Level (B1), which requires approximately 350 hours of English-language study. At this level, learners should be able to cope with language used in a range of everyday situations in their own or a foreign country and to communicate satisfactorily with both native and non-native speakers of English. They should also be able to deal with texts like street signs, public notices, forms, brochures, instructions, city guides, short personal messages such as e-mails and Post-it messages, informal letters, newspaper articles, weather forecasts, etc. The PET syllabus is designed to reflect the use of language in real life and takes a communicative approach to learning English, without neglecting the need for clarity and accuracy.

A large number of colleges and universities as well as employers recognise PET as an official measurement of language competence. The majority of candidates are in Europe and South America. Most of them are full-time students and attend exam preparation classes. On average they have studied English for about four years before taking the exam. PET is usually available six times a year on fixed dates in March, May, June (twice), November and December.

Revised PET Examination – Overview

Paper 1   Reading/Writing   1 hour 30 minutes

Reading – Five parts test a range of reading skills with a variety of texts, ranging from very short notices to longer continuous texts.

Test focus – Assessment of candidates' ability to understand the meaning of written English at word, phrase, sentence, paragraph and whole-text level.

Writing – Three parts test a range of writing skills.

Test focus – Assessment of candidates' ability to produce straightforward written English, ranging from producing variations on simple sentences to pieces of continuous text.

Paper 2   Listening   30 minutes (approx.)

Four parts ranging from short exchanges to longer dialogues and monologues.

Test focus – Assessment of candidates' ability to understand dialogues and monologues in both informal and neutral settings on a range of everyday topics.

Paper 3   Speaking   10–12 minutes per pair of candidates

Four parts. In Part 1, candidates interact with an examiner; in Parts 2 & 4 they interact with another candidate. In Part 3, they have an extended individual long turn.

Test focus – Assessment of candidates' ability to express themselves in order to carry out functions at Threshold level. To ask and to understand questions and make appropriate responses. To talk freely on matters of personal interest.

For further information about PET, visit the Cambridge ESOL On-Line website: www.cambridge-efl.org

© Bloomsbury Publishing 2003. For reference see *Basic English Dictionary* (1-901659-96-8)

How to use your *Basic English Dictionary*

How to use your *Basic English Dictionary*

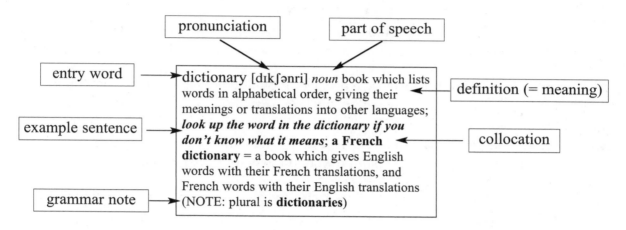

The main features of the *Basic English Dictionary* are:

- Each word has a part of speech label (e.g. noun, verb, adjective). For a list of the parts of speech, see the Glossary in this workbook (p. ii).

- Where a word has more than one part of speech, each part of speech is numbered 1, 2 etc.

- When a word has more than one meaning the letters a, b, c etc. are used for each new meaning.

- Each entry begins with the base form of the word.

- If the plural of a noun is irregular it is shown in a NOTE, e.g. (NOTE: plural is **dictionaries**).

- There are example sentences for all the possible meanings or uses of a word.

- Compounds made of two or more separate words, e.g. *air force*, are in alphabetical order following the base word (air).

- Grammar notes show you irregular forms and inflections, e.g. irregular past forms or irregular plurals.

- Some words are used as part of a phrase. This is shown clearly in bold type.

- Phrasal verbs e.g. *take away*, *take off*, are shown after the main verb entry (take) as separate entries in alphabetical order.

- The explanations use very simple words, easily understood by learners with a basic vocabulary range.

- Words which are often used together (collocations), e.g. *responsible for*, are shown in bold type and illustrated with an example.

- There are symbols for American (US) or British (UK) English uses of a word.

- Example sentences are set in everyday, typical situations and are simple to understand.

- Pronunciation is shown after each word and uses the International Phonetic Alphabet.

Learner training 1

How to learn & revise vocabulary

a. Look at these statements about learning and revising vocabulary and say if they are true or false. Then discuss your answers with a friend or your teacher.

1. It is better to plan regular self-study than study when you think you've got some free time.
2. You should always work through the units in your vocabulary workbook in the order they appear in the book.
3. It's a good idea to practise saying the new words out loud to see if you can pronounce them.
4. While you are studying a unit you don't need to write down new words in a notebook.
5. Always do your exercises in pencil.
6. It is better to revise for half an hour a week than five minutes a day.
7. You should plan when you are going to work on something, e.g. meaning on Sunday, pronunciation on Monday etc.
8. In order to keep a better notebook give each page a title, e.g. sport, travel, prepositions.
9. You should always record the meaning of every word in exactly the same way.
10. You must only use a bilingual dictionary because it's quicker and easier to look up words.
11. There is more information about the use of a word in a grammar book than in your monolingual dictionary.
12. As soon as you see a new English word in a text, look it up in your dictionary.
13. It is a good idea to record together words which often appear together, e.g. parts of the body.
14. If you look up a word in your monolingual dictionary it helps you to decide which word in your own language is the closest translation in this context.
15. You should only use either a monolingual or a bilingual dictionary, but not both.

b. Organise this list of words into three groups and give each one a title.

> bank, breakfast, careful, coin, cold, cooker, cost, currency, dollar, dreadful, exchange, hopeless, interesting, lamb, meal, mushrooms, salad, small, strawberry, value

c. Does your dictionary help you to answer the following questions?

1. Practice is a noun but what is the verb with the same meaning?
2. What adjectives are formed from hope?
3. Advise is a verb but what is the noun with the same meaning?
4. Is the word cookie used more often in UK English or US English?
5. Is the word Hungarian a country or a language?
6. What is the opposite of lose a match?
7. Is feel a regular or an irregular verb?
8. Can the word leaves be a noun and a verb?
9. What is the opposite of dirty?
10. The nouns product and production are related to the verb produce. What are the differences in meaning?

How to prepare for PET by yourself

Reading

Expand your vocabulary and develop your reading skills by looking at English-language magazines or newspapers and reading articles, advertisements and announcements that you find interesting. Look through stories written in simplified English and choose the ones that you find interesting and that are just a little difficult for you. If you live in a country where English is a foreign language and it is not easy to find English newspapers or magazines, then try to gain access to the Internet. Surfing the Internet can give you the chance to read news items or authentic magazine articles. While reading them, always try to guess the meaning of the new words and then check their meaning in your dictionary.

Writing

Keeping a diary in English, writing letters, postcards, Post-it messages, and short notes, or sending e-mails to English-speaking friends are just a few simple, enjoyable tasks that will help you greatly to improve your writing skills. You will find and learn words that mean something to you. In a letter, an e-mail or a short personal note to a friend you will have the chance to write in English about yourself and about interesting things you have done, or just to communicate pieces of information. In this way, your writing will be real practice for you and not just doing homework or answering exercises.

Listening

You can practise your listening skills and have fun at the same time by watching English-speaking films on TV or on video or even going to the cinema; listening to your favourite English songs; or by listening to the news in English. The best way of course is to go out and try to listen to people talking in English, especially native speakers, if this is possible. Do not miss the opportunity to listen to learning materials on cassette or CD in the classroom or on your own, so that you get used to the different kinds of voices and accents.

Speaking

Try to practise speaking English with a friend who is also learning the language and of course do not miss any opportunity to have a conversation in English with a native speaker, either when you are on holiday or when you meet English tourists in your country. During your English course always take part in pair or group activities. You can even arrange with your classmates to spend time practising talking together in English about your daily lives, your plans and hobbies. You may soon find out that you enjoy it!

Adjectives

'Good+' adjectives and 'bad−' adjectives

You can use more than one adjective to describe something or someone good or bad. It depends how strongly you feel about them. Look at the diagram below

lovely (++)   (very) good (+) + ← OK → (very) bad (−)   awful (−)
wonderful (+++)   terrible (−)
terrific (++++)   dreadful (−)
etc.   etc.

The adjectives in the middle are called 'scale' adjectives and give a general description of something. You can use 'very' before them. The adjectives at the ends of the diagram are called 'limit' adjectives and give an extreme description of something. You can use 'absolutely' before them (but not 'very').

a. Put these adjectives into the 'good' or the 'bad' list. Check their meanings in your dictionary if necessary.

| amazing • brilliant • boring • difficult • fantastic • fascinating |
| fine • great • happy • horrible • interesting • kind |
| lovely • nasty • naughty • perfect • super |

GOOD

_____

_____

_____

_____

BAD

_____

_____

_____

_____

b. Match the 'scale' adjectives on the left with the 'limit' ones on the right which have the same meaning. Write at least one 'limit' adjective for these 'scale' adjectives.

1. big _____   a. awful

2. cold _____   b. boiling

3. happy _____   c. delighted

4. hot _____   d. enormous

5. interesting _____   e. excellent

6. nice _____   f. exhausted

7. not very good _____   g. fascinating

8. small _____   h. freezing

9. tired _____   i. tiny

c. Fill in the gaps below with suitable adjectives. Use some of the ones above or others that you know.

1. I had a(n) _____ time at school today. We ate, danced, and played interesting games.

2. They say the new boss is a very _____ person. He never smiles at anyone.

1

Adjectives

3. It is very _____ of you to help me out in this difficult moment. Thank you.

4. There is _____ traffic in the city centre today. Take the train.

5. I've just had some _____ news! I have finally passed my driving test.

6. She is very well-behaved but her 5-year-old brother is very _____.

7. Julie is more than nice. She is really a(n) _____ person.

8. That's _____! Surely they can't fire you for no reason.

9. Don't cook these eggs. They have been in the fridge for a week and they have a(n) _____ smell.

10. The kids had a(n) _____ opportunity to see wild animals in their natural surroundings in the safari park.

11. Standing there on the top of Mount Etna was a(n) _____ experience for me.

12. Have you ever seen her dance? She's absolutely _____!

Adjectives ending in –ing or –ed

The adjectives ending in –ing describe a person, a thing or situation. The adjectives ending in –ed describe how we feel because of a person, thing or situation.

    Examples: It was a very *interesting* programme – I was very *interested* in the programme.

    I feel *depressed* today because the weather is *depressing*.

---

d. Choose the correct adjective to complete the sentences below.

1. Sue wasn't very good at Maths. I was *surprising / surprised* when he passed the exams.

2. It was very *embarrassing / embarrassed* to find out that I had no money with me at the checkout.

3. I enjoyed the Dracula film last night but my younger sister was *frightening / frightened* by it.

4. I thought it was very *annoying / annoyed* to wait for our order for more almost an hour at the restaurant.

5. The children got very *exciting / excited* with the idea of a holiday in Greece.

---

e. Complete each second sentence so that it means the same as the one before. Use the right adjective form.

1. Most students are frightened of speaking a foreign language.

   Speaking a foreign language is _____.

2. The meeting was so boring that I almost fell asleep.

   I was so _____ that I almost fell asleep.

3. The teacher found her pupils' exam results disappointing.

   The teacher was _____ with her pupils' exam results.

   After 10 years she was _____ with their marriage.

4. I was confused because the instructions were only in Spanish.

   The instructions were _____ because they were only in Spanish.

© Bloomsbury Publishing 2003. For reference see *Basic English Dictionary* (1-901659-96-8)

Adverbs

Adverbs of frequency say how often something happens. They usually come before the main verb or after the verb *to be*. The diagram below shows you.

←——→

always _____   occasionally _____

frequently _____   rarely _____

regularly _____   never _____

sometimes _____

a. What do these adverbs mean? In the diagram above, write them beside the adverbs that they mean the same as.

hardly ever, normally, not very often, now and then, often, seldom, usually

b. The sentences below are all real facts or general truths. Complete them with a suitable adverb.

1. It _____ snows in Russia in winter.

2. The temperature in Egypt _____ falls below zero.

3. People _____ drive on the left side of the road in England.

4. There is _____ heavy traffic in the centre of Athens between 8.00 and 9.00 am.

5. It _____ rains in the desert.

6. Italians _____ cook spaghetti for their meals.

c. Are these sentences true about you? If not, write them out correctly using another adverb of frequency.

Example: *I always have tea at breakfast.*
I sometimes have tea at breakfast* OR *I usually have coffee at breakfast.

1. I normally go to school by train.   _____

2. I occasionally watch TV in the afternoon.   _____

3. I always wear a hat.   _____

4. I hardly ever eat chocolate.   _____

5. I never go to the cinema.   _____

6. I usually drink milk with my lunch.   _____

Adverbs of degree describe how much something is so or not. They usually come before an adjective or another adverb, which describes positive or negative situations.

POSITIVE (+)					OK					NEGATIVE (−)
extremely	very	rather	quite	fairly		a bit	fairly	quite	rather	very	incredibly
incredibly		pretty				slightly			pretty		extremely
absolutely											absolutely

Adverbs

d. Replace the bold italic adverbs to make the first three sentences a little more positive (+) and the last three sentences a little less negative (–). Use adverbs from the diagram above.

1. The new bank manager is *quite* friendly.

2. He's been getting *fairly* good results in his new position.

3. We were *very* pleased with the room service at the Hilton.

4. I liked the flat but I thought the bathroom was *very* small.

5. The food was excellent but the bill was *very* expensive.

6. The film has good actors and wonderful photography but the story is *fairly* boring.

Adverbs of manner say how something happens. They are usually formed by adding –ly to an adjective but there are some irregular ones.

Regular			Irregular	
ADJECTIVES	ADVERBS		ADJECTIVES	ADVERBS
beautiful	beautifully		good	well
terrible	terribly		hard	hard
easy	easily		fast	fast

e. Choose the correct words to complete the sentences.

1. Please speak *quiet / quietly*. I am trying to listen to the news on TV.

2. Be *careful / carefully* when you are driving late at night.

3. I can hardly understand Kay when she speaks so *fast / fastly*.

4. She wants to leave this company because they pay workers very *bad / badly*.

5. I really like Jane because she is always so *polite / politely*.

6. I am *awful / awfully* sorry to hear that you have to move to another town.

7. Why are you so *angry / angrily*? I haven't done anything!

8. Liam is studying *hard / hardly* for his English examination.

f. Complete the sentences with *good* or *well*.

1. They did not play _____ so they lost the game.

2. She plays chess but she is not so _____.

3. Did you sleep _____ last night?

4. Her English is so _____ that most people think she is from England.

5. You did very _____ in the exams. Your essay was very _____.

6. How are your parents? Are they _____?

g. Complete the instructions with suitable adverbs. Use the adjectives in the box below to make the adverbs you need. You can only use each of them once.

angry • careful • direct • firm • immediate • patient
probable • proper • safe • slow • strong • usual

How to Complain

Don't shout! Losing your temper or shouting _____ won't help you. Keep calm, speak _____ but _____ and make it clear that you will not go away until someone listens to you _____. Just shouting at the shop assistant is not enough. Go _____ to the top and ask to see the manager.

If the goods you have bought are not working _____ or are damaged you should get your money back _____. Choose a time when the shop is busy and make your complaint _____ but in a polite way. Take photos of the damaged goods, keep all receipts and guarantees _____ and make copies of any letters you have sent or received.

Seven days is _____ long enough for the shop to reply so wait _____ before making a further complaint. If you are reasonable, you will _____ get a fair amount of money back.

> *Don't forget to keep a record of the words and expressions that you have learned, review your notes from time to time and try to use new vocabulary items whenever possible.*

Comparatives & superlatives

Most adjectives with one syllable form the comparative and superlative by adding –er and –est to the end of the word e.g. *tall – taller – tallest, warm – warmer – warmest.*

Many adjectives with two or more syllables and adjectives ending in –ed and –ing form the comparative and superlative by using *more* and *most* before the adjective.

Example: *useful – more useful – most useful, tired – more tired – most tired*

BUT Adjectives with two syllables that end in –y change the *y* into *i* and then add –er or –est

Example: *easy – easier – easiest*

There are some irregular adjectives which use a completely different word for the comparative and superlative form e.g. *good – better – best*

You can make negative comparisons by using *less* or *least* before adjectives of two or more syllables. For one-syllable adjectives you use *not as . . . as.*

REMEMBER: You can use a comparative to compare two things and say that something is *nicer, more interesting* etc. than all the others in a particular group. You use a superlative to say that something is the *nicest, the most interesting,* etc. of the ones in a particular group.

a. Write the comparative and superlative forms of these adjectives in the correct column below. The first three have been done for you as examples.

angry, cheap, beautiful, boring, clear, cold, comfortable, crazy, difficult, dirty,

energetic, filthy, frightening, high, long, nice, noisy, safe, serious, unhappy

(y) –ier / iest	-er / est	more / most
angry – angrier – angriest	cheap – cheaper – cheapest	beautiful – more beautiful – most beautiful

© Bloomsbury Publishing 2003. For reference see *Basic English Dictionary* (1-901659-96-8)

Comparatives & superlatives

b.   Complete the sentences using the comparative or superlative forms of the adjectives in the list.

| bad • big • crowded • delicious • fast • happy |
| interesting • rich • simple • warm |

1. The weather is too cold in this country. I'd like to live somewhere _____.

2. There were a lot of people in the train. It was _____ than usual.

3. We had an awful time. It was one of the _____ holidays in my life.

4. I am very late. What's the _____ way of getting from here to the station?

5. We need a _____ flat. We don't have enough space here.

6. His job is quite boring. He would like to do something _____.

7. Thank you. It was the _____meal I've had for a long time!

8. Her father left her a lot of money. She is now one of the _____ women in the country.

9. You looked depressed this morning but you look _____ now.

10. The instructions were very complicated. They could have been _____.

---

c.   Correct the mistakes in these sentences. Two of them are correct.

1. Mike's headache is badder today. _____

2. Cars are more faster than they used to be. _____

3. It is much hotter today. _____

4. Last night I went to bed more early than usual. _____

5. Ian is a more good player than me. _____

6. My home cinema is moderner than yours. _____

7. His daughter is as older as I am. _____

8. Laptops are not as expensive as they used to be. _____

9. My new boss is more friendlier than the old one. _____

10. I prefer studying Italian. It's not as more difficult as German. _____

Comparatives & superlatives

d.   Look at the advertisements and complete the sentences below with the comparative or adjective forms of these: *cheap, early, late, new, old, small*. There are several different possible answers for some of the questions.

Chateaux Hotel

Ratings: 4 star

No of rooms: 35

Check-out time: 11.30am

Check-in time: 3.00pm

Year built: 1300

Amenities: Air conditioned, Baby sitting, Balcony, Bar, Bath tub, Bathroom telephone, Fireplace, Hairdryer in room, Iron, In-room movies, Parking, Restaurant, Room service, Shower, Telephone, Toilet, TV, Cable TV

Room Rate Offered: Ranging from £606 to £656 for a suite.

Best Lodge Hotel

Ratings: 3 star

No of rooms: 70

Check-out time: 11.00am

Check-in time: 2.00pm

Year built: 1905

Amenities: Alarm clock, Bar, Coffee maker, Free parking, Golf

Room Rate Offered: From £60 to £74 for a standard room

Deluxe Hotel

Ratings: 4 star AA

No of rooms: 115

Check-out time: 11.00am

Check-in time: 12.00pm

Year built: 1999

Amenities: Adjoining rooms, Baby sitting, Balcony, Bar, Bath tub, Bathroom telephone, Beauty salon, Car rental desk, Coffee maker, Coffee shop, Currency exchange, Games room, Gym, Fireplace, Hairdryer in room, Health club, Jacuzzi, Iron, In-room movies, Laundry service, Parking, Restaurant, Room service, Sauna, Shower, Secretarial service, Swimming pool, Telephone, Toilet, TV, Cable TV

Room Rate Offered: From £140 to £186 for a standard room

1. You can check out _____ in the Chateaux Hotel than in the other two hotels but you can check in _____ in the Deluxe Hotel.

2. The Chateaux Hotel is the _____ and the _____ of the three hotels.

3. The Deluxe Hotel is the _____ of the three but it is not the _____.

4. The Best Lodge Hotel is not very modern but Chateaux Hotel is much _____.

Compound nouns

Formation

A compound noun is made up of two words, which together make a new noun. The two words can be either two nouns or an adjective and a noun e.g. *tin opener* (= *a tool that helps you open a tin*), *toothbrush* (= *a brush for cleaning your teeth*), *dining room* (= *the room where you eat meals*).

One or two words?

Compound nouns are usually written as two words (e.g. *phone call*), but sometimes they are joined by a hyphen (e.g. *half-term*) or written as one word (e.g. *moonlight*). There are no rules for this, so it is best to check it in your dictionary.

Pronunciation

Compound nouns are normally stressed on the first part e.g. <u>film</u> star, but sometimes the stress is on both parts e.g. <u>fire</u> <u>engine</u>. Your dictionary shows the stress on compounds.

Your own compounds

You can often form new compound nouns by changing one part a compound form you already know

> Example: *film/rock/pop star, phone book/box/call.*

a. Dictionary practice

1. Look up the word *headache* in your dictionary.

2. How many compound words from *head–* are there? _____

3. Are these written: (a) as one word; (b) with a hyphen; or (c) as two words? _____

4. How many compounds can you form by using the second part: *–ache?* _____

5. Look up the word *fire* in your dictionary.

6. How many compound words are there? _____

7. Are these written: (a) as one word; (b) with a hyphen; or (c) as two words? _____

8. Look up the word *grandfather* in your dictionary.

9. Is it formed from two nouns or an adjective and a noun? _____

10. How many compounds from *grand–* are there? _____

11. Are these written: (a) as one word; (b) with a hyphen; or (c) as two words? _____

12. How many compounds can you form by changing the first part *grand–* and using one of the second parts? _____

Compound nouns

b. Compound nouns

Make compound nouns by matching words from the box on the left with words from the box on the right. Then write them under one of the topics below.

baby • bank • body • boy • car cash • cheque • ear • grand income • parking • pedestrian rain • sun • swimming • traffic	account • book • children • coat costume • crossing • desk • friend glasses • guard • lights • meter park • rings • sitter • tax

THINGS WE WEAR	PEOPLE	ROADS	MONEY
_____	_____	_____	_____
_____	_____	_____	_____
_____	_____	_____	_____
_____	_____	_____	_____

c. Use the compound nouns from above to complete the following sentences:

1. You have to pay _____ on your salary once a year. It depends on how much you earn.

2. They will come if they can find a _____ to look after their one-year-old son.

3. When I am driving I always wear _____ if it is sunny.

4. Leave your car in the hotel _____ rather than in the street.

5. He always has the same problem at the end of each month: there is no money left in his _____.

6. Don't forget to bring your _____ with you. The beaches are fantastic here!

7. When the _____ are red you must stop. Otherwise you may run into another car.

8. I always try to have the right amount of money to pay before I get to the _____ at the supermarket.

9. She has two _____ now. Jenny, her daughter, had twins last month.

10. It's a good idea to take your _____ with you; it's usually rainy this time of year.

11. He chose a pair of beautiful diamond _____ as a birthday present for his wife.

12. The President and his family were accompanied by two of their _____ when they arrived at the Opera House.

13. If you are going to park the car next to a _____ make sure you have the right money with you.

14. If you are on foot, it is easiest to cross the road at the _____.

15. My_____ gave me a bunch of red roses.

16. When he is travelling, he does not like to pay by cash, so he always has his _____ with him.

---

d. Create a new compound noun by taking a word (the first or the second part) from each compound below. Then mark the main stress on each of the new compound nouns. Use your dictionary to check your answers.

     Example: watercolour: *waterfall*

                    toothbrush: *paintbrush*

---

credit card: _____

ticket office: _____

girlfriend: _____

traffic jam: _____

sunshine: _____

saucepan: _____

dining room: _____

---

e. Choose two or three common words and try to create your own compound nouns from them. When you have two or three possibilities, check in your dictionary to see if your words exist. You can start with the common words:

_____ **paper**   **post** _____

_____ **book**   **air** _____

Don't forget to keep a record of the words and expressions that you have learned, review your notes from time to time and try to use new vocabulary items whenever possible.

© Bloomsbury Publishing 2003. For reference see *Basic English Dictionary* (1-901659-96-8)

Conjunctions & connectives

You can use conjunctions to join two sentences or two parts of a sentence. They help you to show the relationship / connection between the two parts of a sentence. Some basic conjunctions are:

after, although, and, because, before, but, if, or, so, when

If you want to make connections between words and phrases, you can use other connecting words, such as:

also, as well, even, like, only, than, too

a. Use your dictionary and complete the tables with the missing words in order to show their function in a sentence.

Conjunction	Function
and	tells you more
	makes a contrast
	tells you the result
	gives you a choice
	answers the question *'when?'*
	tells you something surprising
	makes a condition
	answers the question *'what happened first?'*
	answers the question *'why?'*

Connecting Word	Function
only	says that something is not very big or not very much
	makes a comparison
	is used after a comparative adjective or adverb
	says something is surprising or unusual
	says something is extra

b. Choose the right word to complete the sentences

1. I stayed at home *and / after / or* watched television.

2. I usually drive to work *so / but / and* I went by bus this morning.

3. Do you want to go out *because / or / if* are you tired?

4. We love films *so / because / although* we often go to the cinema.

5. She sleeps *even / also / only* four hours every night.

6. I like Italian restaurants and my husband loves them *as well / even / only.*

7. I went to bed early *although / because / so* I was tired.

8. She did not get the job *if / because / although* she had the right qualifications.

© Bloomsbury Publishing 2003. For reference see *Basic English Dictionary* (1-901659-96-8)

Conjunctions & connectives

9. He works harder *even / than / like* everyone else in the office.

10. I will lend him the money *when / if/ although* he agrees to return it in a month.

c. Rewrite each of the following sentences so that it means the same as the sentence before it. Use the right conjunction.

1. I didn't know many people in the party but I had a very good time.

    _____ in the party I had a very good time.

2. She had studied very hard and she passed her exams.

    She passed her exams _____.

3. Listen carefully or you won't know what to do.

    You won't know what to do _____

4. We live in the same street. We hardly ever see each other.

    We hardly ever see each other _____

5. He worked in a bookshop for two years. Then he went to University.

    He decided to go to University _____

6. The traffic lights went green. Then they crossed the road.

    They did not cross the road _____

7. You have to speak more slowly or she won't be able to understand you.

    She will be able to understand you _____

8. I had an umbrella so I didn't get very wet.

    I didn't get very wet _____

d. Fill in the gaps with *also, as well, even, like, only, than, too*. Use each only once.

I really enjoy cooking and my husband likes cooking _____. All my family like cooking. _____ my 10-year-old son cooks dinner once a week. He cooks _____ a real chef! _____ my daughter doesn't like cooking at all. They say that I cook better _____ my mother. I _____ like to make my own bread and my own wine _____!

e. All the following sentences are about learning English. Complete them in a logical way.

1. I always write words down in my notebook because _____

2. You should always have a dictionary when _____

13

© Bloomsbury Publishing 2003. For reference see *Basic English Dictionary* (1-901659-96-8)

Conjunctions & connectives

3. You can practise speaking English if _____.

4. You need to revise your notes well before _____.

5. You can buy yourself a personal stereo so that _____.

6. Many students are afraid to speak English although _____.

f. Read this text about the Open University and choose the correct word a, b, c or d for each space.

At the Open University, you get as much support as you personally need. (1) _____ you haven't studied for a while, we'll help you get started. And (2)_____ if you have, you'll still be glad to know that help is always there for you. All you need have is an enthusiasm for your studies (3) _____ a willingness to learn. We have 13 local offices around the UK (4) _____ we will put you in touch with your nearest OU centre from the start. (5) _____ you'll have a personal tutor who is a specialist in the subject you want to study. You can talk over the phone, face to face, via e-mail (6) _____ computer conference. As the course progresses, you can meet and exchange ideas with other students (7) _____. Your tutor will give you regular guidance and assessment (8) _____ you will know how your studies are getting on and you will feel sure about how much you progress. Remember, (9) _____ you join the OU, you're never alone – more students register every year with the OU (10) _____ with any other UK university.

1. a) But	b) If	c) After	d) So
2. a) when	b) although	c) even	d) or
3. a) and	b) so	c) also	d) than
4. a) but	b) because	c) when	d) so
5. a) Although	b) Also	c) When	d) Only
6. a) as well	b) only	c) even	d) or
7. a) as well	b) even	c) than	d) after
8. a) because	b) although	c) so	d) but
9. a) before	b) when	c) even	d) like
10. a) also	b) only	c) than	d) and

14

Countable/uncountable nouns

Countable nouns can have *a/an* or *the* before them. You can use them in the singular or the plural. They are usually followed by a plural verb e.g. *apples, shoes, stairs.*

Uncountable nouns cannot have *a/an* before them and you cannot use them in the plural. You can only use a singular verb with them e.g. *sugar, traffic, furniture.*

Some nouns can be countable with one meaning and uncountable with another

> Example: *a hair / hair, a fish / fish, a glass / glass*

> *Some / Any / Much / Many / A lot of / A few*

You can use *some, any, many* and *a few* with plural countable nouns.

You can use *some, any* and *much* with uncountable nouns.

You can use *a lot of* with both plural countable nouns and with uncountable nouns.

---

a. Are the underlined nouns in the sentences countable or uncountable? Write C or U next to them.

1. Are these **oranges** for you? Yes, I love eating **fruit**. _____

2. Where can I put my **luggage**? Leave it on the **shelf** here. _____

3. My **hair** is getting very long. I need to get it cut. _____

4. There is a lot of **information** you can get from him. _____

5. Malcolm is looking for a new **job**. He's been out of **work** for four months. _____

6. He never has enough **money** at the end of the month. _____

7. I am going to buy a lot of new **furniture** for my new **house**. _____

8. Oh no! There is a **hair** in my **tomato soup**! _____

9. I've had too many **cups of coffee** today. I'll have some **fruit juice** now. _____

10. The **day** was wet and dark in the morning but later we had lovely **weather**. _____

11. Careful! There's broken **glass** on the floor. I've just dropped my **glass** by accident. _____

12. He caught a big **fish** at the lake. His wife will cook it with **vegetables**. _____

13. I was in a hurry this morning. I didn't have **time** for **breakfast**. _____

14. I had some interesting **experiences** while I was in Africa. _____

15. If you want to know the **news** you can read the **paper**. _____

---

b. Are these sentences correct? If not, correct the mistakes.

1. Could you give me some informations about the school?

2. There is usually a better weather in the south of the country.

15

© Bloomsbury Publishing 2003. For reference see *Basic English Dictionary* (1-901659-96-8)

Countable/uncountable nouns

3. I had a lot of homework yesterday.

4. He gave me some very good advices.

5. All the furniture in the house are very old.

6. Are you making a progress with your driving lessons?

7. The news is not very good today.

8. I must find a new accommodation soon.

9. He does a lot of houseworks at the weekend.

10. I've got some sand in my shoe.

11. The taxi driver carried my luggages to the taxi.

12. I'd like fishes and chips for dinner.

c. Put _a / an / the / much / many_ where necessary.

1. It wasn't _____ good idea to bring the children to the party.

2. She is looking for _____ work in London.

3. I haven't got _____ luggage with me. Just this bag.

4. I often go to him for _____ advice. I haven't got _____ experience with computers.

5. Cook _____ spaghetti for 8 minutes. Then serve it with _____ tomato sauce.

6. There are _____ words I don't understand so I'll use _____ dictionary.

7. I'll have _____ omelette with _____ mushrooms, please.

8. Peter is very busy these days. He hasn't got _____ free time.

9. The bank was crowded. There were too _____ people.

10. I had _____ onion soup and _____ bread roll for lunch.

16

Countable/uncountable nouns

d. All the nouns in the list are uncountable in English. Are they countable or uncountable in your language?

accommodation •	countryside •	furniture •	information
m o n e y •	n e w s •	s c e n e r y •	t r a f f i c • t r a n s p o r t

Now complete these sentences with a noun from the list above.

1. It's best to use public _____ to go to the city centre. You won't have a parking problem.

2. It is rather difficult to find cheap _____ in central London. Why don't you stay with some friends?

3. Have you heard the _____ about Allison? She is getting married next week!

4. If you need some more _____ about summer courses you should write to a few colleges in England.

5. We plan to buy a lot of new _____ when we move into our own house.

6. They have just bought a house in the _____ surrounded by the most beautiful _____.

7. He hasn't got much _____ left in his bank account.

8. The new motorway is going to stop some of the heavy _____ going through the city centre.

e. Complete the second sentence so that it means the same as the first in each question.

1. My flat has central heating.

    There _____.

2. Most newspapers have job advertisements.

    There _____.

3. She is making good progress in her English.

    Her _____ getting better.

4. The weather is warm and sunny today.

    _____ warm and sunny day today.

5. The house didn't have any more room for the new furniture.

    There _____ in the house for the new furniture.

6. I had some very depressing news today.

    The _____ very depressing.

Prefixes

Prefixes at the beginning of words can help you understand what the words mean. Sometimes words with prefixes have a hyphen e.g. *half*-brother, sometimes they don't e.g. *un*happy. Always use your dictionary to make sure.

Many prefixes are used to give adjectives, verbs or nouns a negative meaning.

Common such prefixes are: *dis–, il–, im–, in–, ir–, un–* .

Prefixes *dis–* and *un–* used with verbs can have two meanings: they can have a negative meaning Example: *like – dislike* or they can mean the opposite of an action e.g. *lock – unlock*.

Other prefixes can give verbs specific meanings e.g. *mis–* (badly or wrongly), *over–* (too much), *re–* (again).

a.   More than one prefix has the meaning of 'not' in English. Look at the examples below using *il–, ir–, im–, un–*. What do they tell you about the use of these prefixes? For example, what kind of words take the prefix *il–*?

_____

1.   It is ***illegal*** to serve alcohol to people under 16.

2.   You can try and read the letter but his handwriting is almost ***illegible***.

3.   His payments are very ***irregular***.

4.   Her age is ***irrelevant*** if she can do the job.

5.   People get very ***impatient*** when they drive in big cities.

6.   It's ***impossible*** to do all this work in two hours.

7.   My bedroom is often ***untidy***; I leave my clothes all over the floor.

8.   We have had some ***unofficial*** meetings with people from the ministry.

b.   **Use the right prefix to make these words opposite. Use your dictionary if necessary.**

_____ agree	_____ lock	_____ formal	_____ happy
_____ employed	_____ legal	_____ honest	_____ understand
_____ visible	_____ regular	_____ dressed	_____ like

c.   **Answer these questions using the words above which have the same meaning.**

1.   She doesn't have a job, does she?

No, she is _____.

2.   Your desk is always in a mess, isn't it?

Yes, it is _____.

3.   He can never wait for longer than five minutes, can he?

No, he is very _____.

© Bloomsbury Publishing 2003. For reference see *Basic English Dictionary* (1-901659-96-8)

4. Driving too fast in the city is against the law, isn't it?

   Yes, it is _____.

5. Didn't you understand the question correctly?

   No, I _____.

6. You cannot see the entrance to the cave from here, can you?

   No, it is _____.

7. Has she taken off her clothes?

   Yes, she is _____.

---

d. Match the common prefixes on the left with their meaning on the right.

1. ex– _____   a. again
2. dis– _____   b. 50% of something
3. half– _____   c. incorrectly
4. in–, im–, il– _____   d. not (usually with adjectives)
5. mis–_____   e. not (usually with verbs)
6. re– _____   f. not (usually with adjectives or verbs)
7. un– _____   g. was but not now

---

e. Use the prefixes above and the words in the box to make words which can complete the sentences correctly.

appear •	comfortable •	lock •	organising •	packed
possible •	slept •	understood •	way •	wife

1. It was _____ to sleep because of the noise.

2. She lives _____ between Oxford and London.

3. Plastic seats are very _____ in hot weather.

4. Many species of plants and animals _____ every year.

5. My _____ and her new husband live abroad.

6. She _____ the instructions and answered two questions instead of three.

7. The department is in a terrible mess. It needs_____.

8. He finally managed to _____ the door and we were able to get inside.

9. We _____ as soon as we got to the hotel and then we went to the beach.

Prepositions

You can use *at, on, in* to describe the place or position of something like this:

at a point/place: ✶   *in* an area/space: ✶   *on* surface: (✶)

These prepositions form pairs of opposites:

up ↑   down ↓

into ↓   out of ↑

over/above ⊤   under/below ⊥

in front of ⊢   behind ⊣.

Many verbs and adjectives are followed by certain prepositions. You should learn these as you meet them e.g. *listen to, wait for, good at*

Some verbs have different meanings if they are followed by different prepositions. Always use your dictionary to check them.

> **Example: look after, look for, look at**

a.   Fill in the gaps with *at, on, in*.

1. I'll meet you _____ the train station.

2. He is British but he lives _____ Italy.

3. She sat _____the bed and read the letter.

4. I left my keys _____ home.

5. There is a lot of snow _____ the ground _____ our street.

6. She is a nurse. She works _____ the General Hospital.

7. They live _____ a very nice house _____the end of the street.

8. Is there any milk _____ the fridge?

9. Leave the books _____ the desk, please.

10. Would you like to sit _____ this table?

b.   Underline the correct word(s) to complete the sentences.

1. Don't stand *in front of / over* me. I can't see.

2. We are flying *up / over* Paris now. Can you see the Eiffel Tower *behind / below* us?

3. My flat is on the first floor. There two more floors *above / under* me.

4. I was driving *in front of / behind* a red car. I could see the number plates.

5. He took off his clothes and fell *into / out of* the water.

6. They began walking *up / over* the hill. They wanted to visit the castle at the top.

20

Prepositions

c. In the sentences below each verb is followed by a gap. Decide if you need to put a preposition or not. If yes, then fill in the gaps with the right preposition. You can use your dictionary.

1. She lived _____ Paris when she was a young girl.

2. Please can you pass _____ me the sugar?

3. What time does the ferry arrive _____ the island?

4. The customer was very annoyed and asked _____ the manager.

5. I am taking _____ my driving test on Friday morning.

6. No one is allowed to enter _____ the room before the end of the meeting.

7. What time did you get _____ last night?

8. She likes listening _____ classical music while she is studying.

9. They have not reached _____ Oxford yet.

10. Will you take the dog _____ a walk?

11. You can stay _____ some friends until you find a place of your own.

12. Don't worry. I'll look _____ your plants while you're away.

13. Someone has taken _____ my mobile phone. I can't find it anywhere.

14. Put _____ your scarf and gloves. It's very cold today.

15. If I'm a bit late, can you wait _____ me?

d. This is what someone said to children who had just arrived at a camp. Choose the correct word A, B, C or D to fill in each gap.

"Welcome to Funway Sports Camp. Before you split (1) _____ groups, let me give you some information (2) _____ the plans for this week. During your time here you will take part (3) _____ twelve different sports activities. (4) _____ the mornings there is a planned programme, but we offer you a choice (5) _____ afternoon activities. You need to sign a list before midday today, saying which sport you are interested (6) _____ You will see the list of activities (7) _____ the wall just as you come (8) _____ the changing rooms. Now, clothes. You can wear your tracksuit (9) _____ most sports but remember to bring shorts and a T-shirt as well in case it's hot. Make sure you have two pairs of sports shoes (10) _____ you, too."

Prepositions

1. a. from   b. into   c. out of   d. at

2. a. for   b. to   c. about   d. of

3. a. into   b. on   c. at   d. in

4. a. On   b. In   c. At   d. From

5. a. of   b. for   c. from   d. about

6. a. about   b. in   c. for   d. after

7. a. in   b. on   c. over   d. at

8. a. on   b. up   c. below   d. out of

9. a. with   b. for   c. in   d. about

10 a. on   b. for   c. with   d. from

e.   Answer these questions about yourself. Then ask another person the same questions to find out about him/her.

1. What are you afraid of? _____

2. What are/were you good at school? _____

3. What are you looking forward to? _____

4. Who/What did you get angry with last week? _____

5. What are you proud of? _____

6. What kind of books are you interested in? _____

7. What different kinds of food are you used to eating? _____

8. Do you belong to any clubs? _____

9. What do you usually complain about? _____

10. What kind of sports are you keen on? _____

Suffixes

Suffixes are used at the end of words to form new words. They help you to change word class i.e. nouns from verbs or adjectives, etc. Some common noun suffixes are:

–ment, –(t)ion → to make nouns from verbs e.g. *improvement, education*

–ness, –ity → to make nouns from adjectives e.g. *happiness*

–er, –or, –ist → to make nouns from verbs or other nouns in order to describe people and their jobs e.g. *manager, writer*

–able, –al, –ful, –ible, –ive, –less, –ous, –y → to make adjectives from nouns or verbs e.g. *famous, cloudy, helpful*

a.   Match the nouns on the left with their meanings on the right.

1. arrangement _____   a. a person who plays football (noun)

2. darkness _____   b. that seems never to end (adjective)

3. endless _____   c. quite sure that something will happen (adjective)

4. film director _____   d. the study of numbers and shapes (noun)

5. footballer _____   e. putting into an order (noun)

6. hopeful _____   f. no light (noun)

7. impressive _____   g. a person in charge of making a film (noun)

8. mathematics _____   h. a person who paints or draws (noun)

9. organization _____   i. so good that impresses

10. artist _____   j. a group of people who work together for the same purpose (noun)

b. Make nouns from the verbs or adjectives in the list and write them in the correct column below.

| amuse • digest • discuss • enjoy • govern • happy • impress |
| inform • invite • measure • popular • prepare • protect • punish |
| responsible • revise • sad • state • suggest • televise |

-ity	-ment	-ness	-(at)ion

© Bloomsbury Publishing 2003. For reference see *Basic English Dictionary* (1-901659-96-8)

Suffixes

c. Choose eight of the nouns from (b) to fill in the gaps in the sentences below.

1. We had a _____ about working hours in the meeting.

2. I mostly watch _____ in the evening.

3. He needs to do his _____ for the History exam tomorrow.

4. This coat doesn't give you any _____ from the rain.

5. Could you give me some _____ about the train times?

6. Can I make a _____? Let's have pizza tonight.

7. Teachers usually have to do a lot of _____ before each lesson.

8. I'm sorry but I'm not free this weekend. I have an _____ to a party.

d. Write down the name of the person who does these things:

1. sing   _____   6. art   _____

2. employ   _____   7. act   _____

3. farm   _____   8. manage _____

4. dance   _____   9. drive   _____

5. direct   _____   10. train   _____

e. The suffix -*ful* often means '*full of*' + the meaning of the adjective and the suffix –*less* means '*without*' + the meaning of the adjective.

Which of these adjectives can form an opposite with –*ful*? Check them out in your dictionary.

careless • endless • helpless • hopeless • painless • useless

Now use a –*less* adjective to describe these people or things. You can use some of the adjectives above or you can guess others. You can use the same adjective more than once.

1. He is a very bad driver.   He is _____

2. That girl is so stupid!   She is _____

3. This bottle opener doesn't work at all!   It's _____

4. This injection didn't hurt me.   It was _____

5. It seems that housework never ends. It's _____

f. Use three –*ful* adjectives and two –*less* adjectives to describe yourself.

_____

_____

_____

24

Word partners

Word partners or collocations are words that are very often used together in the English language. They can be very different in your own language so you need to learn them if you want to use English naturally. They can be combinations of:

Verbs and Nouns: *take a photo, make a noise*, etc.

Adjectives and Nouns: *strong coffee, heavy traffic*, etc.

Common adjectives can go together with many different nouns.

Adverbs and Adjectives: *terribly sorry, fully aware*, etc.

You can use adverbs which mean *very* before certain adjectives to emphasise their meaning.

Prepositions and Nouns: *by mistake, on holiday etc.*

It is best to learn these as *fixed expressions* as there are no rules why a particular preposition goes with a certain noun.

a. Match the verbs on the left with their partner nouns on the right. Use your dictionary if necessary.

VERBS	NOUNS
1. ask _____	a. the bus
2. do _____	b. the car
3. get off _____	c. care
4. have _____	d. a company
5. make _____	e. exercise
6. run _____	f. fun
7. start _____	g. a mistake
8. surf _____	h. a question
9. take _____	i. the truth
10. tell _____	j. the Internet

b. Fill in the gaps with the missing verbs. Be careful to use the right verb form.

1. It was very difficult to _____ the car because there was a lot of snow on our street.

2. Please _____ me the truth about what really happened.

3. You should _____.more exercise and eat less, the doctor said.

4. 'See you soon Bob. Have a good trip and _____ care!' my dad said.

5. She was _____ the Internet for the best e-shopping websites.

6. He is finding it difficult to _____ the company after his father's death.

7. The children _____ a lot of fun playing with the dog.

8. If you don't understand something, you can _____ a question.

9. You'll _____ a mistake if you give him your phone number.

10. You should always wait for the bus to stop before you _____.

© Bloomsbury Publishing 2003. For reference see *Basic English Dictionary* (1-901659-96-8)

Word partners

c. Write two more nouns that you can use with each of the adjectives below in order to make common collocations. Use your dictionary if necessary.

strong	heavy	hard	dry	great
tea	traffic	examination	weather	success
_____	_____	_____	_____	_____
_____	_____	_____	_____	_____

d. Fill in the gaps with a suitable adjective from the ones above.

1. He used to be a _____ smoker but he managed to give it up easily.

2. There is a _____ smell of burning. Is there a fire somewhere?

3. There was _____ rain all day so they cancelled the concert.

4. I had a _____ mouth and I was very hot. How I needed a drink!

5. We had a _____ time in Rome. It was one of my best holidays!

6. Although he has lived in London for a long time he still speaks with a _____ northern accent.

7. With a bit of _____ work and a lot of enthusiasm we can finish it in time.

8. 'Why don't we hire a car? – That's a _____ idea!'

9. Let's have _____ white wine with the starters.

10. It was a very _____ decision for him to leave his job.

e. Use the adverbs in the box to replace _very_ in the sentences below. Use your dictionary to find the right collocations.

absolutely • awfully • completely • highly • really • extremely

1. We should try the new Chinese restaurant. It is _very_ recommended.

2. It is _very_ difficult to work in these conditions.

3. Are you _very_ sure that you have paid the water bill this month?

4. I am _very_ sorry I am late but the buses were on strike this morning.

5. What's he doing? Is he _very_ crazy?

6. I feel _very_ hungry. Is there anything to eat?

f. Rewrite the sentences by replacing the italic words with a preposition + noun phrase. Use the words in brackets at the end of the sentences.

    Example: I took your keys _because I thought they were mine._ (mistake)

    I took your keys by mistake

1. There are two million people _without a job_. (work)

2. He did all the work _without any help from others_. (himself)

3. I can't answer the door now. I'm _making a telephone call_. (phone)

4. She opened the box _because she thought it was for her_. (mistake)

5. I met her yesterday _but it was not planned_. (chance)

6. I am afraid I'm very busy _right now_. (moment)

Words you may confuse

The same word can have more than one different meanings.

a. Look at the entry of the word *light* in your dictionary. How many different meanings does it have as a verb, as an adjective and as a noun?

light [laɪt] **1** *noun* **(a)** being bright, the opposite of darkness; *I can't read the map by the light of the moon* **(b)** electric bulb which gives light; *turn the light on – I can't see to read*; *it's dangerous to ride a bicycle with no lights* **(c) to throw light on something** = to make something easier to understand; **to come to light** = to be discovered **2** *verb* to start to burn, to make something start to burn; *he is* trying to get the fire to light; *can you light the candles on the birthday cake?* (NOTE:**lighting – lit** [lɪt]) **3** *adjective* **(a)** not heavy; *I can lift this box easily – it's quite light* **(b)***(colour)* pale; *he was wearing a light green shirt* **(c)** having a lot of light so that you can see well; *it was six o'clock in the morning and just getting light* (NOTE: **lighter – lightest**)

b. Look at the sentences and decide if the word light is a verb, a noun, or an adjective in each one. Then decide which of the meanings shown above it has.

1. There is more light near the window. It's sunny today. _____

2. Will you light the fire tonight? _____

3. Please turn the light off before you leave the room. _____

4. She has light brown hair and green eyes. _____

5. They left early in the afternoon while it was still light. _____

6. I can carry both bags; they are quite light. _____

7. The police hope that she may throw some light on the case. _____

8. That car hasn't got its lights on. _____

There are words that sound the same but they have a different meaning and a different spelling.

Example: quiet / quite.

quiet [ˈkwaɪət] *adjective* **(a)** without any noise; *can't you make the children keep quiet – I'm trying to work!*; *the hotel said that the rooms were quiet, but ours looked out over a busy main road* **(b)** with no great excitement; *we live in a quiet little village* (NOTE: **quieter – quietest**)

quite [kwaɪt] *adverb* **(a)** more or less; *it's quite a long play*; **(b)** completely; *you're quite mad to go walking in that snow*; *the work is not quite finished yet* **(c) quite a few** *or* **quite a lot** = several, many; *quite a few people on the boat were sick*

c. Look at the two dictionary entries above and complete the example sentences.

1. Please keep _____. The baby is sleeping.

2. The film was _____ interesting but the actors were very bad.

3. They found a table in a _____ corner of the bar.

4. Are you _____ sure you want to go?

5. There are _____ a few emails for you today.

Words you may confuse

There are words that have the similar or related meanings but they are used in a different way. It is a good idea to use your dictionary to check their use e.g. *lend / borrow, job / work*.

d. *Do, Make, Have* or *Take*? Correct the mistakes in these sentences. Two of the sentences are correct.

1. Has she done many mistakes? _____
2. They did a lot of noise during the party. _____
3. Can I take a photo of you? _____
4. Are you making an exam tomorrow? _____
5. We must do a decision soon. _____
6. She always makes her washing at the weekends. _____
7. I always have a shower when I get up. _____
8. Why don't you have a taxi? It's late. _____
9. Susan is making a baby in two months. _____
10. Does he make his homework every day? _____

e. Match the verbs on the left with the words on the right. All the verbs have to do with *talking*.

1. answer _____   a. the bill
2. ask _____   b. lies
3. ask for _____   c. Merry Christmas
4. discuss _____   d. many languages
5. reply to _____   e. a friend about your problem
6. say _____   f. building a new school in the village
7. speak _____   g. someone to help you
8. talk about _____   h. the door
9. talk to _____   i. an email
10. tell _____   j. your problem with your friend

f. Choose the correct word in each of the following sentences.

1. If you lose / loose your passport you must tell your Embassy.
2. She fell / felt and broke her arm.
3. The passport officer checked / controlled my passport.
4. Her husband is a very good cook / cooker. He used to be a chef.
5. Why don't you bring / take your boyfriend with you? We'd love to meet him.
6. Will you borrow / lend me your car for tomorrow?
7. It's a lot of hard job / work looking after children.
8. My father learnt / taught me to swim when I was four years old.
9. I haven't studied hard. I expect / wait I'll fail the exams.
10. The National Bank was robbed / stolen yesterday.
11. It's quiet / quite cold today. I fell/felt it this morning when I was waiting for the bus.
12. He did / made a lot of money when he worked in the cinema.
13. I had / took a burger with salad for lunch.
14. He managed to brake / break the world record again.
15. Can you remember / remind me to pay the water bill by the end of this month?

© Bloomsbury Publishing 2003. For reference see *Basic English Dictionary* (1-901659-96-8)

Modal verbs

Modal verbs are not like other verbs in English. They do not have different forms and they are always followed by a main verb e.g. *I can play tennis and he can play too.*
They do not use *do* or *did* to form questions, negatives or short answers e.g. *He won't not come tonight, will he?*
These are the basic modal verbs in English:

>   can, could, may, might, must, ought to, shall, will, would, should

You can also use *need to* and *have to* as modal verbs.

Each modal verb can have more than one meaning. Always use your dictionary to decide which meaning is used

>   e.g. *I can play football.* **(know how to – ability)**
>   *Can I have a cup of tea, please?* **(I want – polite request)**

a. Look at the dictionary entry of the modal verb *may*. How many meanings can you see?

>   may   [meɪ] *verb used with other verbs* **(a)** *(to mean it is possible)* **take your umbrella, they say it may rain (b)** *(to mean 'can', 'it is allowed')* **guests may park in the hotel car park free of charge (c)** *(asking questions in a polite way)* **may I ask you something?**

b. Decide which meaning of *may* is used in the following sentences.

1.   May I use your phone? _____
2.   I may be going to Italy in the summer. _____
3.   You may only borrow books for two weeks. _____
4.   I think I may have a cold. _____
5.   You may be right. _____
6.   It's getting dark. It may rain. _____

c. Match the sentences on the left with the use of the modal verbs on the right.

1.   You must have a passport if you are travelling out of the country. _____   a. advice
2.   Could you carry this bag for me? _____   b. not allowed
3.   You have to be eighteen before you vote in the UK. _____   c. no need
4.   Travellers should check the weather forecast before leaving. _____   d. impossible
5.   Children needn't bring any food. There is plenty. _____   e. obligation
6.   You mustn't park on a double yellow line. _____   f. permission
7.   Students may leave their clothes in the changing room. _____   g. request
8.   I can't get a ticket for the concert. They are all gone. _____   h. rule/law

d. Complete the sentences with a word from the list. Some of the sentences have more than one correct answer.

>   must • mustn't • should • shouldn't • have to • don't have to • may • might

1.   If you feel tired you _____ go to bed early.
2.   You _____ pay extra if your luggage is more than 20 kilos.
3.   If you want to go climbing you _____ buy some boots.

Modal verbs

4. 'Do you think Simon will come?' 'Who knows? He _____ do'.

5. You _____ worry about me. I'm alright.

6. You _____ pay to join the college sports club. It's free.

7. All UK travellers to Brazil _____ have a visa.

8. You _____ go surfing if you don't know how to swim.

9. 'You _____ start writing now' said the teacher.

10. If you have a heart problem you _____ smoke.

e. Complete the second sentence so that it means the same as the first. Use the right modal verb and any other necessary words.

> **Example: It is essential for passengers get on board by 8.45am.**
> **Passengers *must get* on board by 8.45am.**

1. It is very important that you check in your luggage an hour before your flight.
    You _____ your luggage an hour before your flight.

2. Smoking is not allowed in the doctor's waiting room.
    You _____ in the doctor's waiting room.

3. It is necessary for all employees to learn to use a computer.
    All employees _____ to use a computer.

4. It is a good idea to book a table in advance.
    You _____ a table in advance.

5. We do not allow students to have visitors after 10.00pm.
    Students _____ visitors after 10.00pm.

6. Customers are advised to ask for a receipt after paying the bill.
    You _____ a receipt after paying the bill.

7. It isn't necessary to take your own towel to the hotel's swimming pool.
    You _____ your own towel to the hotel's swimming pool.

8. Visitors are allowed to use the school's canteen.
    You _____ the school's canteen if you are a visitor.

9. Passengers with return tickets are obliged to show them to the driver.
    If you have a return ticket you _____ it to the driver.

10. It is essential to register in the office as soon as you arrive.
    You _____ in the office as soon as you arrive.

f. Look at the short texts below. Work with a partner and tell each other what they mean. Use modal verbs.

1. Nothing of value is left in this van at night. _____

2. Please have ready exact fare for your journey. _____

3. Dogs must be on a lead. _____

4. Flight announcements. Please check the flight information screens. _____

5. One tablet three times a day after meals. _____

> **Example: PLEASE KNOCK BEFORE ENTERING   *You must knock before you go in.***

© Bloomsbury Publishing 2003. For reference see *Basic English Dictionary* (1-901659-96-8)

Phrasal verbs

A phrasal verb is a verb followed by one or two adverbs or prepositions.
    Example: *wake up, get on with, look forward to*
The meaning of the phrasal verb is usually very different from the meaning of the verb on its own.
    Example: *look after, give up*

A phrasal verb can have more than one meaning. You should always check the meaning in your dictionary e.g. *pick up the phone / pick up a language*

Phrasal verbs are very common in English. Most of them are informal and used a lot in spoken English e.g. *Did you* **make up** *that story?* (imagine)

In your dictionary, phrasal verbs follow the entry of the main verb and are in alphabetical order.

a. How many phrasal verbs can you form using these main verbs? Use your dictionary to help you.

come	•	give	•	hold	•	make	•	pull	•	run

b. Look at the dictionary entry of the phrasal verb *get on* and match the meanings with the sentences below

> get on   [ˈget ˈɑn] *verb* **(a)** to go inside or
> onto (a vehicle, etc.); ***they got on the bus at
> the bank* (b)** *(informal)* to become old; ***he's
> getting on and can't work as hard as he used
> to* (c)** to get on (well) = to do well; ***she's
> getting on well at college* (d)** to get on with
> someone = to be friendly with someone; ***she
> doesn't get on with her new boss***

1. How are you getting on in your new job?   _____
2. I think we got on the wrong train.   _____
3. Did you know that Niki is not getting on with the new secretary?   _____
4. How old's Craig then? He must be getting on.   _____

c. Fill the gaps with the missing prepositions in order to complete the phrasal verbs in the sentences below. Use your dictionary.

1. I'll find _____ the name of the restaurant.
2. It took her a long time to get _____ her illness.
3. She is always nervous when the plane takes _____.
4. He told me to carry _____ until the traffic lights.
5. My alarm didn't go _____ and I overslept this morning.
6. He's fallen _____ with his lessons because he's training hard for the basketball game.
7. Can you deal _____ this order please?
8. She broke _____ the engagement two weeks before the wedding.
9. He was driving his new sports car very fast just to show _____.
10. Can you send _____ the doctor? Mum's not feeling well.

d. Fill the gaps with the missing verbs in order to complete the phrasal verbs in the sentences below.

1. Could you _____ _____ after the baby for me while I go to the supermarket?
2. What time does your plane _____ off?
3. Prices have _____ up three times this year.

Phrasal verbs

4. I hope I'll _____through the exam next week.

5. Can you _____ up the radio please? I can't hear it.

6. If you get the shirt in grey colour, it'll _____ well with your trousers.

7. I'm afraid the printer has _____ out of ink. You can't use it now.

8. I would _____ up smoking if I were you. Your voice sounds terrible.

9. The gun _____ off in the boy's hands while he was playing with it.

10. Can you hear this noise? Something's _____ on next door.

11. If you don't remember his phone number _____ it up in the phone book.

12. Maria is not _____ on well with her landlady.

13. Where did you _____ up this funny accent?

14. The police let him go but warned him to _____ out of trouble.

15. This job is perfect for you. Don't _____ it down.

16. The notice said:'_____ off the grass'.

17. 'Can you _____ me through to Mr Potter's room please?' she asked the operator.

18. Can we _____ off our meeting until next week? I am very busy this weekend.

19. _____ out! There is a big truck coming your way!

20. _____ up! We'll miss the plane.

e. Read A's remarks and questions and complete B's answers with suitable phrasal verbs. Use the verbs in the box. Use the verb *turn* twice.

hang • put • switch • take • tidy • turn (×2) • wake

1. Your coat's on the floor.   B: *OK, I'll hang it up*

2. A: Is Michael still asleep?   B: Yes, I'll _____

3. A: Your desk is a horrible mess!   B: OK, _____

4. A: This light is too bright.   B: OK, _____

5. A: There's a good film on TV.   B: OK, _____

6. A: Is your cigarette still burning?   B: Yes, _____

7. A: Is the rubbish still in the kitchen? B: Yes, _____

8. A: This music is too loud.   B: OK, _____

f. Complete the sentences so that they make sense.

1. I grew up _____

2. Two men tried to break into _____

3. I have to go to the garage to pick up _____

4. As soon as she came in she took off _____

5. She promised to pay back _____

6. I can't get over _____

7. I asked him to sort out _____

8. You can leave out _____

9. He usually forgets to get off _____

10 You can put on _____

Verb forms & verb patterns

Some verbs need to have another word (an object) after them: transitive verbs
Some other verbs do not an object after them: intransitive verbs

   Example: *Put* the book *on the table.* BUT *Please stay.*

Sometimes a verb must be followed by other grammar words or patterns, like

Verb + object	e.g. *Let's discuss the plan.*
Verb + object + question word	e.g. *He asked me where to find her.*
Verb + object + infinitive	e.g. *They told us to wait outside.*
Verb + that	e.g. *I suggest that you go alone.*
Verb + object + that	e.g. *She warned me that it was expensive.*

a. Can you describe the verb patterns in these sentences? Match the underlined parts on the left with the verb patterns on the right.

1. He didn't **tell me why** she was leaving.	a. verb + no object
2. The receptionist **confirmed my reservation**.	b. verb + object + infinitive
3. They **insisted that** we stay with them.	c. verb + object + question word
4. You could **send her some flowers**.	d. verb + object
5. Do you **want me to leave** the room?	e. verb + two objects
6. Can you **move** please?	f. verb + that

b. Correct the mistakes in these sentences. Two of them are correct.

1. I would like that you leave.

2. Can I apologise my mistake?

3. Please explain me what to do.

4. He suggested me to tell the police about it.

5. I insist you to come.

6. Did you say that the bank was closed?

7. We discussed about my report at the meeting.

8. You never showed me how the video works.

9. Can you persuade her coming to the party?

10. Please tell I am very busy.

c. Complete these sentences so that they make sense.

1. It was getting too cold in the room so I suggested _____

2. We had to read the book for homework and then discuss _____

3. If you don't understand the instructions, I will explain _____

4. She wasn't feeling well, so I advised _____

5. I didn't know the way but he showed _____

33

Verb forms & verb patterns

Some verbs are followed by another verb in an *–ing* **form e.g. enjoy dan*cing*, avoid drin*king.***
Some verbs are followed by another verb in a *-to infinitive* **form e.g. want *to stay*, hope *to be* ....**
Some verbs can be followed by either *–ing* **or** *-to infinitive* **form e.g. like *doing/to do* something**

d. Choose the correct verb forms to complete the sentences.

1. She decided *to study / studying* abroad.

2. Have you finished *to use / using* the photocopier?

3. He hopes *to finish / finishing* his report by the end of next week.

4. Do you enjoy *to live / living* in the country?

5. I finally managed *to pass / passing* my driving test.

6. I asked him to carry my bags but he refused *to help / helping*.

7. Can you imagine *to work / working* on TV?

8. You should avoid *to drive / driving* in the city centre between 8.00am and 10.00am.

9. She promised *to let / letting* me know the results as soon as possible.

10. Did you remember *to buy / buying* him a present? It's his birthday tomorrow.

e. Complete this letter with the verbs in the box. Put them in the right form *-to infinitive* **or** *–ing***; use two of the verbs twice.**

become • bring • change • come • drive (×2) • learn
leave • let • meet • see (×2) • slow • tell • write • work

Dear Charlotte,

Thank you for your lovely letter. It was great to hear from you. My news is that I've decided (1) _____ jobs. I finish (2) _____ at Thompsons in two weeks and I am starting with my new company on 1st April. Thompsons didn't want me (3) _____ but Martins, the new company, offered me more money and more prospects for a career. I hope (4) _____ a manager in less than a year.

By the way, I forgot (5) _____ you that I'm learning (6) _____. You see, I am going to drive a lot around the country and the company offered (7) _____ me use one of their cars. It wasn't easy at first because I wanted (8) _____ everything quickly. My teacher said I was a bit dangerous on the road and advised me (9) _____ down. Now I even enjoy (10) _____!

Well, I'm having a party on the 23rd and I'd love (11) _____ you. Most people won't be there before 9.00 but if you feel like (12) _____ earlier you're very welcome. And you must promise (13) _____ your new boyfriend.

I would really like (14) _____ him.

I've got to stop (15) _____ now and rush off to work.

Looking forward to (16) _____ you on the 23rd.

Lots of love, *Anne*

Animals & pets

a. Put the names of these animals into the right column. Some of them can go into more than one column.

ant •	bear •	bee •	butterfly •	camel •	cat •	cow • dog
donkey •	eagle •	fly •	giraffe •	goat •	goldfish •	hamster
hen •	horse •	lamb •	lion •	monkey •	mosquito •	parrot
pig •	rabbit •	robin •	sheep •	spider •	snake •	tortoise

FARM ANIMALS	WILD/ZOO ANIMALS	INSECTS/BIRDS	PETS
		ant	

b. Complete these sentences with a suitable animal from exercise _a._ above. There may be more than one correct answer.

1. _____ can eat leaves from tall trees.

2. _____ usually obey human commands.

3. _____ can imitate human speech.

4. _____ are large female farm animals kept to give milk.

5. _____ provide us with wool.

6. _____ make honey.

7. _____ shed their skin several times a year.

8. _____ are large wild animals of the cat family.

c. Match each animal with its young.

ANIMAL			YOUNG
cow	•	•	piglet
hen	•	•	kid
goat	•	•	chick
pig	•	•	lamb
sheep	•	•	calf

d. Read the text about dogs as pets and fill the gaps with the right word A, B, C or D

The right dog for you

Buying a dog (0) _____ a very big responsibility and one of the (1) _____ important decisions that any family has to make. A dog is for (2) _____ and it will become your concern

Animals & pets

for the next ten years at least. Before you rush out into getting one, consider first if and how it will fit into your lifestyle and what you can give it in return. Being a dog (3) _____ can be extremely rewarding. But don't forget that your furry friend will need regular (4) _____, feeding, grooming and most of all companionship. You must be ready to set aside some time every day to look after it and (5) _____ with it.

When we (6) _____ a dog into our family we want it to be liked by everyone who comes to our home, whether they are friends, our children's friends or visitors on business. We don't want our new family (7) _____ to be annoying to us or anyone else either in the car or when we are (8) _____ it for a walk in the street or in the countryside. Our dogs have to (9) _____ good behaviour and we have to teach them. We should use a lot of repetition, we should watch out for instinctive behaviour which we must control, and we should teach the dog to trust us. We must try to understand (10) _____ the dog's senses work and find a way to control them.

0. a. one	b. is	c. has	d. does
1. a. more	b. very much	c. most	d. much
2. a. now	b. living	c. life	d. always
3. a. buyer	b. lover	c. companion	d. owner
4. a. exercise	b. food	c. game	d. treatment
5. a. train	b. play	c. teach	d. exercise
6. a. grow	b. buy	c. take	d. own
7. a. animal	b. member	c. creature	d. visitor
8. a. bringing	b. getting	c. taking	d. letting
9. a. learn	b. be	c. educate	d. behave
10. a. if	b. when	c. which	d. how

e. Answer the following questions for yourself. Then discuss them with a friend.

1. Which of these would you choose as a pet? Why?

goldfish • hamster • kitten • puppy • monkey • rabbit • tortoise •

2. Which of these animals do you think are most useful for humans? Why?

dog • cow • horse • hen • sheep • bee • elephant • camel

3. Which of these animals would you not like to meet? Why?

tiger • shark • snake • lion • spider • bat

British & American English

British English is spoken mainly in the United Kingdom while American English is spoken mainly in the USA. Although they are the same language, there are some differences in spelling, pronunciation, grammar and vocabulary.

Many common words we use or see every day are different in British and American English. Or the same word can have a different meaning.

You can use both British and American English for international communication. If you are taking a British examination, like KET or PET, you can use either British or American English but you should do it consistently.

In your dictionary you will find a lot of information about words that are used in American or British English with different meanings and words that are spelled differently. Most words are given only one pronunciation, which is acceptable in British and American English.

---

a. Which of the following words are British and which are American English? Write Br E or Am E next to each one.

apartment _____	cookies _____	motorway _____	trainers _____
autumn _____	elevator _____	pants _____	trousers _____
biscuits _____	fall _____	parking lot _____	truck _____
cab _____	French fries _____	rubbish _____	vacation _____
candy _____	garbage _____	semester _____	wardrobe _____
car park _____	highway _____	subway _____	
chips _____	lift _____	sweets _____	
closet _____	lorry _____	toilet _____	

---

b. Complete this table.

British English	American English
_____	candy
_____	two weeks
chips	_____
_____	vest
petrol	_____
pavement	_____
_____	sneakers
football	_____
crisps	

---

c. Look at these pair of words. Which is the British spelling and which is American spelling? Use your dictionary to make sure.

1. color – colour
2. traveler – traveller
3. dialog – dialogue
4. centre – center

5. meter – metre
6. license – licence
7. labor – labour
8. cancelling – canceling

British & American English

d. Which of the following words are pronounced differently in British and American English?

tomato   zebra

peach   bicycle

schedule   favour

ballet   rubber

e. Underline the correct word in the following sentences. First you have to decide if the speaker is using British or American English.

1. You can put your trainers in the *wardrobe / closet.*

2. Throw the garbage into the *trashcan / bin.*

3. You bake the *biscuits / cookies* in a baking pan for 30 minutes.

4. Lorries drive very fast on the *highway / motorway.*

5. Last summer we spent *a fortnight / two weeks* on a Greek island during our vacation.

6. Your *rubber / eraser* is next to the Scotch tape on your desk.

7. The new *semester / term* at St Catherine's secondary school starts in a week.

8. I always leave the car in a car park and take the *underground / subway* to the centre.

9. Her apartment is on the fourth floor but she never uses the *elevator / lift.*

10. I try not to eat snacks like *sweets/candy* or crisps at the office.

11. You can see your *timetable / schedule* on the bulletin board.

12. This *waistcoat / vest* will look great with your new trousers.

f. The text below is written in American English. Rewrite it using British English.

It was a warm day in the fall. I had been driving along the freeway since eight in the morning. Now it was getting near lunchtime and I needed to fill up the car and get something to eat. So I drove toward the nearest town, left the car in a parking lot by the highway and took a cab to the center. I started walking around and it was getting quite hot. Then I saw a nice little diner with tables out on the sidewalk. I had a hamburger with salad and French fries and drank a cool beer. I started talking with a truck driver who told me where to find a gas station. I thanked him and looked for a phone booth to call my wife. It was really a nice break.

_____
_____
_____
_____
_____
_____
_____
_____
_____
_____
_____
_____
_____
_____
_____
_____
_____
_____
_____
_____
_____

38

a. All the words in the box describe things we wear. Write them into the correct column. Use your dictionary. Some of them can go into more than one column.

belt • boots • cap • cardigan • coat • dress • earrings
gloves • jacket • jeans • jumper • hat • overalls
pyjamas • ring • sandals • scarf • shirt • shoes
shorts • skirt • socks • suit • sunglasses • sweater
T-shirt • tie • tights • tracksuit • trainers • trunks • vest
waistcoat • watch

HEAD	CHEST	LEGS	FEET	WHOLE BODY	ACCESSORIES

b. Use some of the words above to label these pictures.

1. _____ 2. _____ 3. _____ 4. _____

5. _____ 6. _____ 7. _____ 8. _____

Clothes

c. How many combinations can you make from the words below?

    Example: warm leather gloves

| a | warm
thick
long
short
thin | woollen
cotton
silk
leather
silver
gold | belt
boots
gloves
coat
jacket
scarf
necklace
T-shirt
socks
tie
earrings
skirt
trousers | _____
_____
_____
_____
_____
_____
_____
_____
_____
_____ |

d. Fill the gaps with a verb in the box in the right form. You can use some verbs more than once.

> get changed • get dressed • get undressed • put on • take off
> try on • wear

1. 'Should I _____?' I asked. 'Not completely' said the doctor, 'Just _____ your shirt.'

2. After a quick shower she _____ and had a cup of coffee. It was a little cold, so she _____ her coat before she left home.

3. I wanted to _____ a nice blue jacket I saw in the shop window. But it looked a bit small. Then the shop assistant noticed that I was _____ a thick sweater. So I _____ my sweater and the jacket felt very comfortable.

4. You'd better _____ . You can't _____ your office suit to the party!

5. She got home very late. She _____ her raincoat, threw it on the floor, _____ and went straight to bed.

e. Write down:

1. Five things that only women usually wear: _____

2. Five things that men and women usually wear: _____

3. Five things you don't like wearing: _____

4. Five clothing items you have in your wardrobe: _____

Communications

a. Write the words in the box into one or more of the columns below. Each column describes a way of communication.

channel • daily • dial • e-mail address • envelope • headlines address • journalist • inbox • keyboard • message • mouse mobile • phone book • phone number • postbox • postcode post-it • remote control • satellite dish • screen • stamp the 10 o'clock news • weather forecast

LETTERS/MEMOS	TELEPHONE & FAX	E-MAIL	NEWSPAPERS & MAGAZINES	TV & RADIO

b. Look at the newspaper headlines. What kind of news are they? Choose from the list below. The first one has been done for you.

a. sports news   b. business news   c. book review   d. world news   e. home news   f. feature

1. **GOVERNMENT TO CLOSE 2,000 POST OFFICES**   _e. home news_

2. **AMERICA TO SEND IN MORE TROOPS** _____

3. **TIME TO SPRING CLEAN YOUR BUSINESS** _____

4. **FOOTBALL AROUND THE WORLD** _____

5. **PAPERBACK: NORMANDY BY PATRICIA FENN** _____

6. **HOW FAR WILL YOU GO TO BUY A HOME** _____

Communications

c. Match the TV & Radio programmes on the left with their descriptions on the right.

1.	International news	_____	a. Football cup final
2.	Nature programme	_____	b. Pedro decides to marry Sonia
3.	Quiz show	_____	c. Reports from all over the world
4.	Soap opera	_____	d. Film of elephants in Africa
5.	Sports programme	_____	e The prize for correctly answering all the questions is £1m

d. Fill the gaps in the phone conversations below. Use these verbs or phrases. You will need to use them in the right form.

> speak • call • leave • put through • is that • be afraid
> be back • give • return • have got

1. A: Good morning. Denton Electronics

   B: Oh good morning. Could I _____ to Mr Clark, please?

   A: Who's _____ please?

   B: My name is Paula Marsden. Mr Clark tried to _____ to me earlier but I was out of the office. So I am _____ his call.

   A: Right, Madam. I'll _____.

2. A: Hello?

   B: Hi. _____ Maria?

   A: No. I _____ Maria is not here at the moment.

   B: Oh. Do you know when she'll _____ ?

   A: No, I'm not sure.

   B: OK then. Could I _____ a message for her?

   A: Yes, of course.

   B: Could you ask her to _____ me a ring later this evening?

   A: Sure. What's your name?

   B: I'm Julie. We are in the same English class. She _____ my number.

   A: Right Julie. I'll tell her.

   B: Thank you. Bye.

   A: Bye.

Computers, e-mail & the internet

a. Use the words in the box to label the pictures below. They are all about computers.

monitor • screen • keyboard • mouse • CD-ROM drive
laser printer • laptop • floppy disk

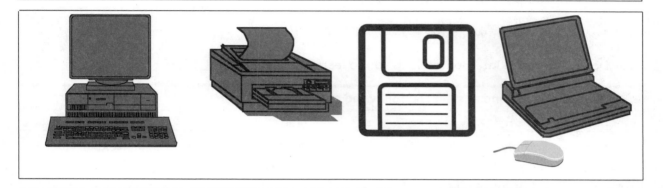

b. You can do different things by clicking your mouse on different icons on your computer screen. Match the symbols with the words they mean.

1.	a. cut
2.	b. copy
3.	c. open a new document
4.	d. save
5.	e. print
6.	f. open an existing document
7.	g. paste
8.	h. check spelling

c. Complete these common computer related words.

1. hard _____

2. laser _____

3. lap _____

4. _____ net

5. key _____

6. ____-line shopping

7. web _____

8. _____-ROM

9. floppy _____

10. a _____ processor

11. e- _____

12. a print _____

13. net _____

43

Computers, e-mail & the internet

d. Answer these questions for yourself. Then ask someone else.

1. Do you have a computer at home? What type? _____

2. Do you use computers at work/school? What for? _____

3. Do you find most computers easy to use? _____

4. Do you use e-mail? What for? _____

5. Do you think the Internet can help you to learn more? _____

e. Look at this e-mail and answer the following questions.

Reply	Reply All	Forward	Delete	Previous	Next

From: claire@lanet.co.uk
To: tess@skymail.com
Cc: keith@skymail.com
Subject: new e-mail address
Attached: schooladdresses.doc (21.5KB)

Hi Tess,

Thanks for the new address. I have saved it in the address book and hope we can keep in touch. Life is frantic as usual and lots of things happening. I'm moving into a new house on Saturday.

How are you and Keith? What are you doing these days? I had dinner with Keith in Frankfurt, which was great fun.

Regarding work, I have attached the list of addresses you wanted.

Looking forward to hearing from you soon.

Best wishes,
Claire :☺

1. Where do you write the e-mail address of the person you are sending an e-mail to?
    _____

2. What is the e-mail address of the sender of this e-mail?
    _____

3. Is anyone else going to receive a copy of this e-mail? What's his/her e-mail address?
    _____

4. Can you see a few words that say what the e-mail is about?
    _____

5. Is the sender happy or unhappy? How does he/she express it?
    _____

6. Is there a computer file attached to this e-mail?
    _____

Education

a. All the words below describe objects you can find in a classroom. Use some of them to label the pictures below.

board • cassette • chalk • computer • desk • drawing pin
file • glue • notebook • noticeboard • pencil • rubber • ruler
satchel • scissors • textbook • timetable • whiteboard marker

1._____ 2._____ 3._____ 4._____ 5._____ 6._____ 7._____

b. Complete these pair of words. You usually find them together in the classroom. One has been done for you.

1. student   +   _teacher_

2. chair   + *d* _____

3. marker   + *b* _____

4. drawing pin   + *n* _____

c. Match the subjects on the right with the topics on the left. One has been done for you.

1. Architecture	a. the First World War
2. Art	b. human bones
3. Business Studies	c. swimming
4. Chemistry	d. drawing
5. Geography	e. light and heat
6. Information Technology	f. $\sqrt{4} = 2$
7. History	g. governments of the world
8. Languages	h. Latin American countries
9. Maths	i. computers
10. Medicine	j. design of buildings
11. Physical Education	k. H_2O
12. Physics	l. the one-minute manager
13. Politics	m. French grammar

d. Which of the subjects above do you usually study at university and not at school?

Education

e. The words in the box are about student life. Match them with their explanations below

degree • full-time course • lectures • term • sports centre • student card

1. where several different sports can be played _____

2. something you can use to prove that you are a student _____

3. the qualification you get at the end of university _____

4. studying all day from Monday to Friday _____

5. teachers at university _____

6. part of the student's year _____

f. Read the information about an English language course and choose a b c or d to fill the gaps.

If you (0) ____*d*____ an adult aged 18 or more you are welcome to (1) _____ our International Summer Course in English Language. We (2) _____ the course between Saturday June 29th and Saturday August 17th. You can enrol for a course of two weeks or more at any time during this period. The course will take place on the premises of one of the oldest (3) _____ in Oxford University. It stands in the centre of the University area and has two hundred and ninety undergraduates and one hundred and sixty graduate students during the (4) _____ year.

During the course you will (5) _____ fifteen classroom hours per week learning English as a foreign language. You will also have an hour session per week (6) _____ British culture and history. There will be a maximum of twelve students per class. On the first Monday of the course we will (7) _____ you a test and interview in order to place you to an appropriate level of class.

During the course you will be given all teaching material and you will be able to (8) _____ the college's Internet facilities. You will mostly practise your speaking and listening (9) _____ while your class teacher and the director of studies will monitor you on an individual basis. When you complete the course successfully you will receive a (10) _____ of attendance.

0. a. be	b. have	c. were	d. are
1. a. take	b. have	c. study	d. learn
2. a. participate	b. attend	c. offer	d. start
3. a. colleges	b. schools	c. universities	d. classrooms
4. a. school	b. calendar	c. academic	d. teaching
5. a. access	b. learn	c. be	d. have
6. a. learning	b. studying	c. teaching	d. practising
7. a. give	b. write	c. take	d. pass
8. a. practise	b. borrow	c. use	d. join
9. a. ability	b. skills	c. knowledge	d. results
10. a. degree	b. diploma	c. licence	d. certificate

Entertainment

a. Write the words in the box into the right column. Some of the words can go into more than one column.

actor • artist • band • cartoon • classical • composer
concert hall • director • exhibition • film • gallery • guitar
musical • musician • novelist • opera • orchestra • rock group
painter • play • poetry • pop group • producer • sculpture
singer • songwriter • stage • violin

MUSIC	ART	LITERATURE	CINEMA	THEATRE

b. Match the words/phrases in the two columns.

THINGS TO SEE/GO TO			PLACES TO GO	
1. paintings	•	•	a.	concert hall
2. a concert	•	•	b.	a museum
3. a film	•	•	c.	an art gallery
4. an opera	•	•	d.	a cinema
5. an exhibition	•	•	e.	an opera house
6. a play	•	•	f.	a theatre

c. Complete the sentences with the verbs in the box in the right form.

appear • go to • listen to • play • read • sing • see • watch

1. Do you prefer to _____ the cinema or _____ TV?

2. Did Brad Pitt _____ in *Mission Impossible*?

3. She likes to _____ classical music when she wakes up.

4. I went to _____ the *Lord of the Rings*. Now I want to _____ the books.

5. They _____ in front of 6,000 people who had come to _____ their favourite rock group.

6. The pop star could dance very well but he couldn't _____. We could hardly hear him.

7. The orchestra _____ Beethoven's ninth symphony.

47

Entertainment

d. Read the sentences about these famous people. What are/were they?

1. Mozart wrote a lot of symphonies. He was Austrian. _____

2. Shakespeare wrote a lot of plays. He lived in England in the 16th century. _____

3. Steven Spielberg has made very popular films like *ET*, *Jurassic Park*, and *Jaws*. _____

4. Britney Spears is American and has made some very successful song albums. _____

5. Picasso painted pictures. His most popular work was *Guernica*. _____

6. Elizabeth Taylor was born in Britain, lived in Hollywood and played *Cleopatra*. _____

e. Match the descriptions of the books below with one of the kind of books.

1. a cookery book	•	•	a. Some children are frightened by a ghost.
2. a travel book	•	•	b. A girl falls in love with her teacher.
3. a history book	•	•	c. It's a made-up story.
4. a horror story	•	•	d. It's called 'How to cook the best pasta'.
5. a detective story	•	•	e. It's about a real journey to the Amazon.
6. a romantic novel	•	•	f. It's about the Olympic Games.
7. a science fiction story	•	•	g. It's called 'Lions in the Jungle'
8. a book about animals	•	•	h. It describes how the police catch a murderer.
9. a book about sports	•	•	j. It's about Napoleon's last days.
10. a historical novel	•	•	k.It's about aliens living with people.

f. Answer the following questions about yourself. Then ask a friend.

1. What is your favourite kind of entertainment? _____

2. Who is your favourite film star? _____

3. Do you enjoy watching horror films? Why (not)? _____

4. What do you like to read most? _____

5. How much does a cinema ticket cost in your country? _____

6. Is your country famous for any particular kind of entertainment? _____
   If so, what is it called? _____

48

Environment

topics

a. What can you see around you in the countryside or in the town? Write a C or a T next to these words to indicate which you mostly find in the countryside and which in a town.

1.	bank	9.	hedge	17.	sand
2.	bush	10.	hills	18.	sea
3.	car park	11.	lake	19.	shops
4.	cottage	12.	library	20.	stream
5.	farm	13.	museum	21.	town hall
6.	fields	14.	path	22.	valley
7.	forest	15.	pebble	23.	wild flowers
8.	grass	16.	river	24.	waterfall

b. What can you do in the countryside? Match the verbs or phrases on the left with the 'countryside' words on the right.

1.	go skiing	• •	a. in the sea
2.	have a picnic	• •	b. up the mountain
3.	hear	• •	c. the flowers
4.	go swimming	• •	d. pebbles
5.	smell	• •	e. by the lake
6.	pick up	• •	f. the wind blowing
7.	walk	• •	g. down the slope
8.	climb	• •	h. in the forest

c. Match the names of places on the left with the words on the right to make true sentences.

1.	The Alps	*is / are*	• •	a. a continent
2.	The Mediterranean	*is / are*	• •	b. a country
3.	Italy	*is / are*	• •	c. a desert
4.	The Nile	*is / are*	• •	d. a forest
5.	The Atlantic	*is / are*	• •	e. a group of islands
6.	Africa	*is / are*	• •	f. a jungle
7.	The Bahamas	*is / are*	• •	g. an island
8.	The Sahara	*is / are*	• •	h. a mountain
9.	Everest	*is / are*	• •	i. a mountain range
10.	The Black Forest	*is / are*	• •	j. an ocean
11.	The Amazon	*is / are*	• •	k. a river
12.	Cyprus	*is / are*	• •	l. a sea

49

© Bloomsbury Publishing 2003. For reference see *Basic English Dictionary* (1-901659-96-8)

Environment

d. Look at the words below and decide which are good or bad for the environment. Put a tick (√) or a cross (×) next to each one of them.

acid rain	( )	factories	( )
recycled paper	( )	bottle banks	( )
litter	( )	sprays	( )
solar panels	( )	conservation	( )
traffic jam	( )	chemicals	( )
bicycles	( )	ozone layer	( )
global warming	( )	exhaust fumes	( )

e. What should or shouldn't we do in order to protect the environment? Use the verbs in the box to complete the two columns below.

> cut down • destroy • plant • protect • recycle • save
> throw away • waste

WE SHOULD

_____ tropical rainforests
_____ more trees
_____ paper
_____ endangered species
e.g. pandas

WE SHOULDN'T

_____ energy
_____ plastic bags
_____ trees
_____ forests

f. Use the words in the box to complete the text about the environment.

> climate • fossil fuels • energy • gas • global warming • oceans
> planet • poorer countries • sources of energy • storms

As we enter the 21st century one third of the people on the (1) _____ cannot use electricity for basic needs such as lighting or cooking. One of the most serious problems today is to get people clean and reliable (2) _____ so that they can have clean water, health care facilities, heating and lighting. (3) _____, which is caused by burning fossil fuels, threatens people's lives around the world. The world's poorest people use very little of the world's oil, coal and (4) _____ but they will suffer most from floods and (5) _____ if no action is taken. Whole countries in the Indian and Pacific (6) _____ are threatened by flooding as the sea level rises. If we are going to stop the earth's (7) _____ getting out of control, we should stop using most of the world's (8) _____ such as coal, oil and gas to produce energy. It's time to change to alternative sources of energy, like using the (9) _____ of the wind and the sun, both at home and all around the world. We mustn't forget that (10) _____, where 80% of the world's people live, cannot afford oil, coal and gas.

© Bloomsbury Publishing 2003. For reference see *Basic English Dictionary* (1-901659-96-8)

Family & relations

a. Look at the family tree below. Imagine you are Michael and, using the words in the box, describe the relationship between you and:

1. Mary – She is my _____
2. Edward – He is my _____
3. Jessica – She is my _____
4. Rebecca – She is my _____
5. Emma – She is my _____
6. Dorothy – She is my _____
7. Jack – He is my _____
8. John – He is my_____

9. Hilary – She is my _____
10. Andrew – He is my _____
11. Sarah – She is my _____
12. Rory – He is my _____
13. Peter – He is my _____
14. James – He is my _____
15. Christine – She is my _____

> niece • granddaughter • grandmother • sister • son • grandfather
> grandson • mother • uncle • father • aunt • nephew • daughter
> brother • wife

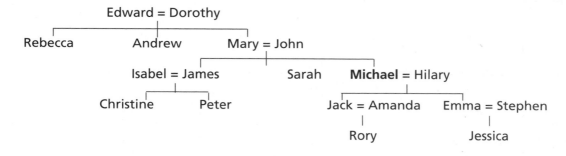

Key
=: married to

b. Fill the gaps with the missing words or phrases

> old friend • divorced • first name • get a divorce • get married
> have a baby • only child • single • single parent family • surname

1. When you are born, your family gives you a _____, like *Mary* or *James*.

2. John is just a(n) _____. We haven't seen each other for 10 years.

3. We grew up in a(n) _____ family. Our mother never lived with us.

4. She is pregnant. She's going to _____ next July.

5. He is _____ now but he still sees his ex-wife.

Family & relations

6. We're engaged and planning to _____ in the summer.

7. Their marriage has too many problems. They are going to _____.

8. I am a(n) _____ I have no brothers or sisters.

9. Both my sisters are married with children but I am still _____.

10. Her first name is Anne, but I don't know her _____.

c. Match the beginnings with the right endings to make logical sentences about Francesca's life.

1. Francesca was born •   • a. for six months
2. She grew up •   • b. her village to work at the local hospital
3. Her first boyfriend •   • c. with another student doing medicine
4. She went out with him •   • d. in her late twenties
5. She went to University •   • e. as soon as she got her degree
6. She fell in love •   • f. in a car accident.
7. They got married •   • g. in 1968
8. She had a baby •   • h. once she had finished school
9. Her husband was killed •   • i. was Mario, a boy from school
10. Francesca went back to •   • j. in a small house by the sea.

d. Answer these questions about yourself

1. What is your first name? _____

2. Do you have a middle name? _____

3. Are you an only child? _____

4. Who is your best friend? _____

5. What is your surname? Is that common in your country? _____

6. Have you got any colleagues or close friends who speak English? _____

Food & drink

a. Look at the foods in the box and put them into the right column. Use your dictionary to check their meaning.

apples • bananas • bacon • beef • beetroot • beans • biscuit
cauliflower • carrot • cherry • chicken • chocolate cake • duck
fruit   salad • grapes • ham • cream • lamb • lemon
melon • mushrooms • onions • oranges • pepper • pork
potato • salmon • sardines • sausages • steak

meat	fish	fruit	vegetables	dessert

b. How many words of fruit and vegetables can you find in this puzzle? The words may be horizontal, vertical or diagonal.

S	T	O	R	E	T	G	R	A	P	E
P	E	P	P	E	R	A	N	N	I	S
E	L	M	O	T	I	R	U	E	N	T
C	A	U	L	I	F	L	O	W	E	R
A	N	S	T	R	C	I	T	H	A	A
R	O	H	B	E	O	C	H	S	P	W
R	A	R	E	N	O	P	A	N	P	B
O	G	O	I	W	E	E	S	O	L	E
T	R	O	D	A	P	A	D	I	E	R
I	N	M	R	E	S	C	U	F	O	R
M	E	L	O	N	C	H	E	R	R	Y

Food & drink

c. Which is the odd one out in each of these groups? Why?

1.	salmon	veal	beef	lamb	_____
2.	yoghurt	cheese	egg	ice cream	_____
3.	beans	mushroom	cauliflower	peach	_____
4.	chicken	duck	pork	turkey	_____
5.	tea	orange juice	coffee	beer	_____

d. You usually buy food and drink in containers e.g. *packets, jars* etc. Match the food and drink words on the right with their containers on the left. Some can be linked with more than one container.

1. some bottles of _____

2. a bag of _____

3. some cans of _____

4. a carton of _____

5. a jar of _____

6. a packet of _____

a.	beer	g.	honey	n.	spaghetti
b.	chewing gum	h.	jam	o.	sugar
		i.	milk	p.	sweets
c.	coffee	j.	olive oil	q.	tea
d.	Coke	k.	orange juice	r.	water
e.	fish	l.	pears	s.	wine
f.	flour	m.	rice		

e. Answer these questions to find out about your eating habits. Then ask one or two more people.

1. Do you usually fill up your plate with too much food? _____

2. Do you drink many fizzy drinks like Coca Cola or Sprite? _____

3. Do you have snacks like cakes, biscuits or chocolate? _____

4. Do you often eat at a fast food restaurant? _____

5. Do you enjoy eating foods like chips, crisps and peanuts? _____

Use the following scores to find out if you eat healthily.

YES/OFTEN = 3   SOMETIMES = 2   HARDLY EVER = 1   NEVER = 0

HOW DID YOU SCORE?

12 or more: Perhaps you are eating too much of the wrong kind of food!
6–10:   You are generally careful about what you eat.
0–5:   Are you going hungry?

f. This is part of a letter you received from your English friend Mike.

I usually have cereal and milk for breakfast and a sandwich or a salad for lunch. At about seven o'clock I have dinner with my mum. And at the weekends I eat out with friends.

Now write a letter to Mike, telling him about your eating habits.

© Bloomsbury Publishing 2003. For reference see *Basic English Dictionary* (1-901659-96-8)

Free time, leisure & hobbies

a. Put these words/phrases into the right column. The columns describe different types of leisure activities and hobbies. Some of the words/phrases can go into more than one column.

antiques • board games • camping • cards • chess
listening to CDs • coins • cooking • DIY • gardening
hiking • hunting • jogging • painting • photography
playing the violin • playing computer games • reading
rock climbing • scuba diving • stamps • surfing the Internet
tennis • watching videos • window shopping

Activities at home	Outdoor activities	Things people collect	Creative hobbies

b. Read what these people say about their favourite hobbies and activities and decide which is their hobby. Choose from the ones above.

1. I have great fun going round shops and markets looking for a bargain.

2. I really enjoy preparing exotic dishes and I usually try new ideas. I feel very proud when people want to have more.

3. I try to practise every day but it disturbs my neighbour too much. You see, I have to play the same thing over and over again.

4. It's a very useful hobby for people like me who have a house but don't want to spend too much money. Actually, I do a better job than many professionals.

5. I don't really like going to the gym. I needed something that would help me keep fit but something that I can do whenever I like. So I usually go early in the morning before going to work.

6. I love watching a good film, especially the ones with my favourite actors. But I prefer to do it in the comfort of my own home.

7. I normally use colour but sometimes you get a better effect with black and white. It depends on the subject.

Free time, leisure & hobbies

c. Match the verbs on the left with the hobbies on the right. Add one or two more words each time to describe more activities.

1.	make	•	• a.	cards, _____., _____
2.	collect	•	• b.	classical music, _____, _____
3.	do	•	• c.	old movies, _____, _____
4.	go	•	• d.	furniture, _____, _____
5.	play	•	• e.	gardening, _____, _____
6.	watch	•	• f.	fishing, _____, _____
7.	read	•	• g.	coins, _____, _____
8.	listen to	•	• h.	comics, _____, _____

d. What do you need to do your favourite free-time activity? Choose words from the box for the following people.

balls	•	brush	•	hammer	•	material	•	nails	•	needle	• net
olive oil	•	paint	•	pasta	•	pins	•	racket	• saucepan	•	scissors
		seeds	•	spade	•	tomatoes	•	watering can			

1. I am going to make a dress to wear at the party next week.

2   I am going to work in the garden for an hour.

3. I am going to cook dinner for my friends.

4. I am going to decorate my bedroom and put up some bookshelves.

5. I am going to play a game of tennis.

e. Answer these questions about yourself. Then ask someone else.

1. What's your favourite free-time activity? Why? _____

2. What do you need to do it? _____

3. Have you got a hobby? What is it? _____

4. Is it an expensive hobby? _____

5. Why do you like it? _____

6. How much time do you spend doing it? _____

7. What are the most popular hobbies in your country? _____

Health & sickness

a. How serious are these health problems? Put the problems into the correct column. Add as many more as you know in the right columns.

| a broken wrist • a cold • flu • hay fever • a heart attack |
| lung cancer • a sore throat • a stroke • toothache |

common problems (not too serious)	aches and pains (more serious)	very serious illnesses

b. Read what this man says to his doctor. Then circle the parts of the body in the drawing below to show the man's problems.

'I've got a terrible headache and my chest hurts. My shoulder aches and my feet hurt. I've got a pain in my knee and my neck hurts. I've got a bad stomach ache and my legs hurt too!'

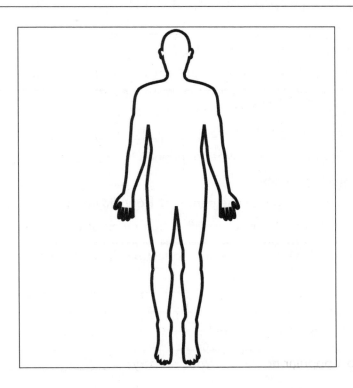

Health & sickness

c. Complete the sentences with a suitable phrase. Use the words in A and B to make suitable phrases.

A
ask
examine
go to
make
stay
take
write

B
an appointment
questions
your chest
these pills
a prescription
in bed
the chemist

1. Could I _____ to see the doctor please?
2. The doctor will _____ about yourself and family.
3. Can you take off your shirt please? I have to _____. said the doctor.
4. You will have to _____ after your meals, three times a day. I'll _____ for this medicine.
5. I want you to _____ for a couple of days and get some rest.
6. I asked my sister if she could _____ and get the medicine for me.

d. Finish the second sentence so that it means the same as the first.

1. She took an aspirin because she wanted to stop her tooth hurting.
   She took an aspirin so _____.
2. If you go swimming you will keep fit.
   Swimming will help _____.
3. Get some fresh air and you'll sleep well.
   If you can't sleep well you _____.
4. It is bad for your heart to eat too much meat.
   Eating too much meat _____.
5. People with flu should stay in bed for a few days.
   If _____ you should stay in bed for a few days.

e. Answer these questions about yourself.

1. Have you ever been travel sick? Where? _____
2. Have you ever been unconscious? What happened? _____
3. Have you ever had a blood test? Why? _____
4. Have you ever had a tooth out at the dentist's? How did you feel? _____
5. Have you ever broken your leg or arm? What happened next? _____

f. Now use the following words to write similar questions in order to ask a friend.

1. burn / hand _____
2. be / hospital _____
3. have / injection _____
4. be / ambulance _____
5. eyes / tested _____

58

a. Complete this vocabulary network with words from the box.

> alarm clock • armchair • bathmat • coffee table book • cupboard
> fridge • kettle • pillow • sheets • shower • sink • sofa
> towels • video • wardrobe • washbasin

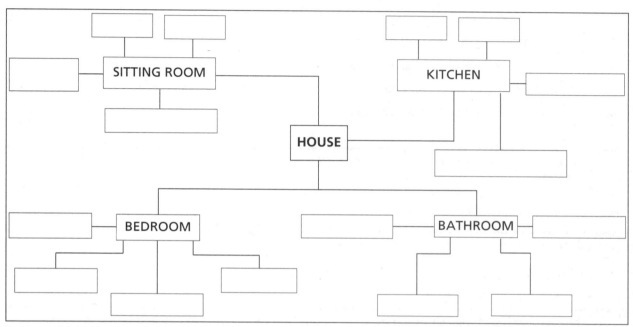

b. Complete the sentences with the missing words. They all describe rooms of the house.

1. The bathroom is where you _____

2. The bathroom is where you have a _____ or a _____

3. A study is where you usually _____ or _____

4. The lounge is where you _____ and _____ or
   _____

5. The kitchen is where you do _____

6. The dining room is where you usually have _____

7. A utility room is where you often have _____

8. A spare room is often where _____

---

c. In which room do you usually _____? Answer these questions for yourself.

1. have breakfast _____

2. listen to your CDs _____

3. feel most relaxed _____

4. think about your problems _____

5. read the newspaper _____

6. Check your emails _____

59

House & home

d. If you don't remember the exact word for an object you see, you can easily describe it if you can answer these questions: What is it made of? What is it used for? What does it look like?

e.g. **It is usually made of wood and you hang your clothes in it : wardrobe**

Match these words with their descriptions below.

| dishwasher • frying pan • chest of drawers • pillow |

1. It is a machine that you usually have in the kitchen and you use it for washing cups, plates etc.

2. It is made of metal and you use it in the kitchen. You can cook an omelette in it.

3. It is usually made of wood and you use it for keeping sheets, towels, clothes etc. separate.

4. It is usually made of feathers and cloth and you find it on the bed. You use for resting your head on.

e. These are some things you can find in the kitchen or the living room. The letters are jumbled. What are they?

1. fsao _____
2. nacitusr _____
3. kocore _____
4. ltteke _____
5. hiamcrar _____

6. bopdacru _____
7. degirf _____
8. edivo _____
9. veon _____
10. partce _____

f. Match the names of types of home or accommodation in the box with the pictures below.

| block of flats • bungalow • caravan • castle • cottage • house • tent |

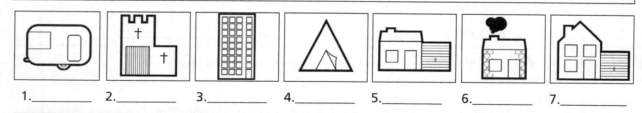

1._____ 2._____ 3._____ 4._____ 5._____ 6._____ 7._____

e. Choose adjectives from the box to describe the rooms and types of homes below.

| convenient • cramped • dark • noisy • quiet • spacious • sunny • untidy |

1. a bedroom with lots of things lying on the floor _____

2. a house in a street with very little traffic _____

3. a flat in the centre of a busy city _____

4. a house with very small windows _____

5. a room with too much furniture _____

6. a house with shops and a school nearby _____

7. a house with large rooms _____

8. a living room that faces south _____

60

Languages, countries & nationalities

Country adjectives are used to describe people's nationality and language. Most common endings are – **(i)an**, **-ish** and **–ese**. e.g. *German, Turkish, Chinese*

There also some irregular country adjectives e.g. *French*

a.   **Complete the table with the missing words. Use your dictionary to find the right words.**

COUNTRY	NATIONALITY	LANGUAGE
Italy		
Brazil		
	Egyptian	
Poland		
		Greek
		Russian
	Welsh	
Spain		
	Argentinian	
United Kingdom		
	German	
Japan		
Portugal		
	Israeli	
The Netherlands		
	Swedish	
		Turkish
	Saudi Arabian	
	Australian	
Mexico		
	French	

b. **Mark the main stress on the words in the box and practise saying them.**

Austria • Australia • Japan • Japanese • Arabic • Italian
Saudi   Arabia • Portuguese • Brazilian • Chinese • Egyptian

c. **Which country is different? Why? Think of the languages they speak there.**

1.   England   Canada   Iceland   New Zealand

2.   Austria   Italy   Switzerland   Germany

3.   Mexico   Spain   Chile   Brazil

4.   Egypt   Morocco   China   Saudi Arabia

5.   Canada   Switzerland   Scotland   France

61

Languages, countries & nationalities

d. Do you know where these capital cities are? Complete the sentences.

1. Lisbon is the capital of _____

2. Seoul is the capital of _____

3. Cairo is the capital of _____

4. Vienna is the capital of _____

5. Madrid is the capital of _____

6. Helsinki is the capital city of _____

7. Lima is the capital city of _____

8. Prague is the capital city of _____

9. Cardiff is the capital city of _____

10. Stockholm is the capital of _____

e. Answer this quiz for yourself first. Then ask a friend.

1. What is the main language that is spoken in South and Central America? _____

2. Which country has New Delhi as the capital city? _____

3. In which country do people speak Mandarin? _____

4. In which country was Mahatma Gandhi born? _____

5. Which country has Buenos Aires as the capital city? _____

6. What language is spoken in Israel? _____

7. How many countries can you name where English is spoken? _____

8. What nationality was Cleopatra? _____

9. In which country people eat a lot of pasta? _____

10. What language is spoken in Russia? _____

Money & numbers

a. Match the words on the left with the numbers on the right.

1.	eight and a quarter	•	• a.	0.35
2.	second	•	• b.	£1m
3.	half a million dollars	•	• c.	£3.25
4.	thirty-five percent	•	• d.	$1,235
5.	one pound fifty	•	• e.	2nd
6.	one million pounds	•	• f.	$500,000
7.	nought point three five	•	• g.	35%
8.	twelve pounds and five pence	•	• h.	£1.50
9.	three pounds twenty-five	•	• i.	8¼
10.	one thousand two hundred and thirty-five dollars	•	• j.	£12.05

b. All the verbs in the box are about money. Use ten of them in the right form to complete the sentences. Use your dictionary to check their meanings.

> borrow • buy • charge • cost • earn • find • give
> lend • lose • pay • save • sell • spend • waste • win

1. Last week a 15-year-old boy _____ $1m in a game on TV.
2. We _____ the house for £125,000 last year but we have already _____ over £5,000 on repairs.
3. His father _____ him £60 as pocket money last week.
4. I'm afraid I've _____ my money on this leather coat because I never wear it.
5. He _____ £35,000 a year in his new job.
6. The new car _____ us £12,000 but we didn't _____ the whole amount at once.
7. She _____ £25 from me and never paid it back.
8. He is trying to _____ money by walking to work rather than taking the bus.

c. Match the beginnings with the endings in columns A and B. One has been done for you.

1.	Can I cash	•	• a. does this shirt cost?
2.	Could I have	•	• b. a bank near here?
3.	How much	•	• c. sign the cheque?
4.	I'd like to pay	•	• d. credit cards?
5.	Where do I	•	• e. for this £50 note?
6.	Do you accept	•	• f. these traveller's cheques, please?
7.	Is there	•	• g. my bill, please.
8.	Could you give me change	•	• h. a receipt, please?

d. Decide where you would ask each of the questions above. At a hotel? In a shop? In the street? In a bank?

1. _____	5. _____
2. _____	6. _____
3. _____	7. _____
4. _____	8. _____

63

e. Rewrite the following sentences using one of the words in the box for each sentence. Each second sentence must have the same meaning as the first one.

afford • borrow • cost • earn • rent • waste

1. How much did you pay for this car?

    How much did _____.

2. My salary is about £32,000 a year.

    I _____ 32,000 a year.

3. They are going to let their flat to us.

    We _____ their flat.

4. Could you lend me your dictionary?

    Can I _____ your dictionary?

5. The trip is too expensive for me.

    I cannot _____ this trip.

6. It's not worth buying.

    It's a _____ of money.

f. Fill in the gaps in the following text with A, B, C or D. The first one has been done for you.

If you travel to London (0)__*B*__ train you can (1) _____ your ticket at the local train station using a (2) _____. At certain times of the day there is a discount on the (3) _____ so you can sometimes get a(n) (4) _____ ticket. It's a good idea to have plenty of (5) _____ with you so that you can use it to (6) _____ for your underground ticket from a machine when you arrive in London. If you don't have the correct (7) _____ you will probably have to queue at the ticket office. Of course you can also go to London by coach. This is not as (8) _____ as the train, although it takes longer. The driver can (9) _____ you a ticket, and it doesn't cost (10) _____ to travel at busy times of day.

0	a. with	b. by	c. on	d. the
1	a. sell	b. buy	c. win	d. pay
2	a. receipt	b. cheque	c. credit card	d. change
3	a. fare	b. ticket	c. cost	d. bill
4	a. economical	b. single	c. expensive	d. cheap
5	a. money	b. change	c. currency	d. exchange
6	a. earn	b. save	c. cost	d. pay
7	a. ticket	b. money	c. currency	d. total
8	a. cheaper	b. more money	c. expensive	d. more
9	a. buy	b. sell	c. offer	d. lend
10	a. money	b. anything	c. extra	d. cheap

64

Opinions & feelings

a. Fill in the blanks to create expressions to describe people's feelings. Some of the words can fit in more than one sentence. Use the correct form of the words on the right.

1. He really _____ football, he plays it every day.
2. She _____ cooking, she prefers to get takeaways.
3. I _____ what we do at the weekend, I'm happy either way.
4. They _____ each other, so they've decided to get married.
5. My mother _____ soap operas, I'm not allowed to watch them at home.

- Love
- Like
- Don't mind
- Don't like
- Hate

b. These are more expressions you can use to describe feelings. With which of the words above are they closest in meaning?

I really like _____

I don't enjoy _____

I'm looking forward to _____

I loathe _____

I'm bored of _____

I sometimes worry about _____

I really dislike _____

I feel very happy about _____

I'm keen on _____

It makes no difference to me _____

c. How do you feel about these things? Use the words above to make true sentences about yourself.

chips _____

_____

cold weather _____

_____

cooking_____

_____

dogs _____

_____

football_____

_____

getting up late _____

_____

learning English _____

_____

pizza _____

_____

playing computer games _____

_____

swimming _____

_____

travelling by train _____

_____

working late _____

_____

d. Complete each second sentence so that it means the same as the first one. Use the words in the box.

| offers • recommends • refuses • suggests • persuade |
| disappointed • feels • enjoys • keen on • thinks |

1. 'I'm sure I'll win the game.'
   He _____ confident about winning the game.
2. 'In my opinion, this trip is a waste of time.'
   He _____ the trip is a waste of time.
3. 'You really should see a doctor about it.'
   She tries to _____ me to see a doctor about it.
4. 'No, I won't sell it.'
   He _____ to sell it.

65

Opinions & feelings

5. 'I really like buying presents.'

   She _____ buying presents.

6. 'Why don't you go to a Greek island?'

   He _____ going to a Greek island.

7. 'This wine is excellent.'

   He _____ the wine.

8. 'Shall I make the salad?'

   He _____ to make the salad.

9. 'I don't really like extreme sports like hang gliding.'

   She is not _____ extreme sports, like hang gliding.

10. 'I hoped I would go swimming today but it's too cold.'

    She is _____ that she can't go swimming.

e. All the words and phrases below describe people's opinions. Put them into the right column.

In my opinion   Maybe, but don't forget . . .
I think   Yes, that's true.
I quite agree   As far as I am concerned
I totally disagree   I think you're right
Personally   I don't think so
According to   You could be right, but . . .

AGREEING	DISAGREEING	GIVING OPINION

f. Rewrite these sentences so that they mean the same as the sentence before them.

1. I don't think you can learn a foreign language in three months.

   In my _____ can't learn a language in three months.

2. Yes, I agree with you.

   Yes, I _____ right.

3. The newspaper says that the President is dead.

   According _____ the President is dead.

4. I don't think it's a very good idea.

   As far _____ isn't a very good idea.

5. You are absolutely wrong, I'm afraid.

   I _____ I'm afraid.

People & descriptions

a. Put the words in the box into the right column. You can use them to describe what people look like.

bald • a beard • beautiful • blonde • curly • elderly
in his early thirties • fair • fat • a fringe • good-looking
green eyes • handsome • long • light brown • medium height
middle-aged • pale skin • petite • plain • a pointed nose
a ponytail • pretty • short • skinny • slim • straight
tall • in his teens • thin • young

General	Face and Head	Height and Build	Age

b. Complete these sentences in a suitable way. There may be more than one correct answer.

1. They've both got blonde _____.

2. She is quite _____, about 1 metre 70, I think.

3. She has wavy red _____ and beautiful green _____.

4. Both men were very good-_____ and fairly _____ – probably in their late twenties.

5. She has long fair _____ and a very pale _____.

6. He keeps his long hair tied back in a _____.

c. Choose three of these famous people and write descriptions of their appearances.

Luciano Pavarotti • Diana, Princess of Wales • Sylvester Stallone • Michael Jackson
President George Bush • Madonna • Nelson Mandela • Eminem • Kylie Minogue

People & descriptions

d. All these adjectives describe people's characters. Which ones describe positive or negative qualities? Which ones can describe both and why?

| aggressive • cheerful • clever • cruel • dishonest |
| flexible • generous • kind • lazy • mean |
| miserable • optimistic • relaxed • pessimistic • reliable |
| strong • stubborn • stupid • tense • unfriendly • weak |

Positive Qualities	Negative Qualities	Both

e. Match the sentences on the left with the character adjectives on the right.

1. _____ always brings you a little present.   •   •   a. lazy
2. _____ never tells the truth.   •   •   b. shy
3. _____ is only interested in himself.   •   •   c. dishonest
4. _____ always smiles and makes a joke.   •   •   d. generous
5. _____ is afraid to speak to strangers.   •   •   e. modest
6. _____ never boasts about himself.   •   •   f. selfish
7. _____ hates spending money.   •   •   g. cheerful
8. _____ never helps with the housework.   •   •   h. mean

f. The adjectives in the two boxes describe people. Find seven pairs of words with similar meanings in box A and seven pairs of words with opposite meanings in box B.

A
blonde • bright • cheerful • clever
easy-going • fair • fat • good-looking
handsome • nervous • optimistic
overweight • relaxed • tense

B
attractive • careful • careless • cheerful
confident • miserable • foolish
hard-working • lazy • shy • strong
plain • weak • wise

g. Which words from this unit would you use to describe yourself? _____

Places & buildings

a. Read what someone says about certain places. Which places are being talked about? Choose from:

a. health club

b. hotel room

c. language school

d. an office

e. a restaurant

f. seaside resort

g. small town

1. It doesn't have a computer room but every classroom has a video.

2. It has its own bathroom with a bath tub and a shower. There is also cable TV.

3. There are fifteen tables in the main area and another ten on the first floor. The bar is open all day.

4. It's a beautiful place with lovely beaches. Unfortunately it's a bit quiet in the evenings.

5. There's a desk with a telephone on it but there is no computer. It's dark with very small windows.

6. There aren't any good cafes and it hasn't got a library. There is only one cinema.

7. It's got modern sports facilities and an Olympic-size swimming pool. You can also have an aerobics class three times a week.

b. Can you unscramble these words? All of them describe places you can find in the town.

1. briraly _____

2. smumue _____

3. nabk _____

4. nowt lahl _____ _____

5. tosp cefifo _____ _____

6. dteeaprsin eonz _____ _____

7. rqaeus _____

8. atrhete _____

Places & buildings

c. Match the words in the box with the places to visit below.

> antiques • arcade • artist • bargains • clothes • drawing • elephant
> exhibition • fence • fruit • giraffe • lions • monkeys
> old CDs • painting • sculpture • souvenirs • stall • vegetables

ART GALLERY	WILDLIFE PARK	MARKET

d. Match names of buildings and parts of buildings with their definitions. Use your dictionary to check your answers.

> attic • balcony • basement • bungalow • front door
> garage • gate • letterbox • pavement • skyscraper

1. a very tall building in a big city _____
2. a room in a building which is under the level of the ground _____
3. a building where you can keep your car _____
4. the path you walk on at the side of the road _____
5. a house with only a ground floor _____
6. a hole in a front door through which letters are delivered _____
7. main door to a house or building _____
8. a small floor sticking out from the upper level of a building _____
9. a room at the top of a house, under the roof _____
10. a low door usually made of wood or metal, not inside a building _____

e. Where would you see the notices below? Match them with the words on the left.

1. In an airport waiting area •   • a   Please do not feed the animals
2. In a library •   • b.   Beware of pickpockets
3. In a bank •   • c.   Do not leave bags unattended
4. On the door of a hotel room •   • d.   Sold out
5. Outside a public telephone •   • e.   Changing rooms downstairs
6. Outside a theatre •   • f.   Silence
7. In a zoo •   • g.   Do not disturb
8. In a department store •   • h.   Out of order
9. On the underground •   • i   Please queue other side

Restaurants & cooking

a. Fill the gaps with the words in the box. One has been done for you.

apertif	•	bill	•	book	•	courses	•	dessert	•	main
		rare	•	starter	•	tip	•	well-done		

Eating out

If you are planning to eat out in a restaurant you often have to (1) _book_ a table, especially if it's a popular place to eat. In most restaurants you usually have three (2) _____ You start with a(n) (3) _____. (e.g. a soup), then you have the (4) _____ course or dish (e.g. steak or chicken), and you can finish with a(n) (5) _____ (e.g. ice cream or fruit salad). If you like you may also have a(n) (6) _____ (e.g. gin and tonic) before the meal and coffee or tea after the meal. If you have steak you can ask to have it (7) _____, medium or (8) _____. When you are ready to pay, you ask for the (9) _____ and sometimes you also leave a (10) _____ for the waiter – 10% is usually enough.

MENU

Broad Bean and Bacon Soup
Prawn and Cucumber Salad
Smoked Salmon Pâté served with Hot Toast

—————

Grilled Plaice Fillet with Spinach
Chicken Thighs with Spicy Tomato Sauce
Pork Fillet in White Wine served with a
Cream Blue Cheese Sauce
Lamb with Cherries and a Mint Sauce
Mushroom Risotto

—————

A selection of Steaks available . . .
Fillet, Sirloin, T-bone
(All served with salad)

—————

Baked apple and coconut pudding
Wine jelly cream with peaches
Double chocolate ice cream

—————

Coffee and Dinner Mints

—————

£ 28.50 per person

---

b. Look at the menu and answer the following questions.

1. How many starters are there? _____

2. Which starter doesn't contain vegetables? _____

3. Which dish may be rare, medium or well-done? _____

4. Which dish contains alcohol? _____

5. Which dessert doesn't contain fruit? _____

6. Which dessert is definitely cooked in the oven? _____

7. Which starter is served cold? _____

8. Would someone who likes mild food select the chicken dish? Why (not)? _____

9. How much is the cost of a meal for a couple? _____

10. Do you have to pay extra for the coffee? _____

71

Restaurants & cooking

c. Fill the gaps in the sentences with the verbs in the box. There may be more than one correct answer.

book • bring • have • made • order • served • show • take • serves

1. Are you ready to _____ now, madam? – Hmm . . . What's Murgh Korma? – It's an Indian dish _____ with chicken, yoghurt and onion and it's usually _____ with rice.

2. Could you _____ the bill please?

3. May I _____ you to your table, sir? The waiter will come to _____ your order in a few minutes.

4. La Strada is my favourite restaurant. I always sit at the same table and the same waiter always _____ me. I always _____ the same dish too: tagliatelle. And I never have to _____ my table before I come.

d. All the verbs on the left (A) describe ways of cooking. Match them with the descriptions on the right (B) and the examples of foods you can cook like this (C).

A			B			C
boil	•	•	in oil or butter above the heat	•	•	e.g. cakes, bread
bake	•	•	in the oven using oil	•	•	e.g. meat, potatoes
grill	•	•	in water above the heat	•	•	e.g. carrots, spaghetti
fry	•	•	in the oven without oil	•	•	e.g. toast, steak
roast	•	•	under the heat	•	•	e.g. chips, sausages

e. Look at the following kinds of food. Do you often eat them cooked in this way in your country? If not, how do you cook them?

1. fried eggs _____
2. raw spinach _____
3. fried bread _____
4. baked potatoes _____
5. raw fish _____
6. fried rice_____

7. baked bananas _____
8. grilled sausages _____
9. roast beef _____
10. fried cheese _____
11. boiled carrots _____
12. fried tomatoes _____

f. Which kind of food or drink are the people talking about in the following sentences? There may be more than one correct answer.

1. It makes you sneeze if it goes up your nose. _____

2. I use it in cooking a lot but it makes your breath smell. _____

3. If you leave it out of the fridge it will melt. _____

4. They make me cry when I chop them. _____

5. I don't normally have any late at night. It doesn't let me go to sleep. _____

6. I always have it well-done. _____

7. It's an alcoholic drink made from grapes. _____

a. Match the types of shop on the left with the items they sell on the right.

1. baker's •	• a.	cigarettes, magazines, newspapers
2. butcher's •	• b.	almost everything
3. bookshop •	• c.	mainly food and household goods
4. boutique •	• d.	bread, cakes, biscuits
5. chemist's •	• e.	meat
6. greengrocer's •	• f.	books, maps, dictionaries
7. newsagent's •	• g.	designer clothes
8. supermarket •	• h.	medicine, baby products, cosmetics
9. department store •	• i.	fruit and vegetables

b. Put the items below in the right column, under the general word which describes the group of items.

apples • bananas • a bookcase • boots • coffee
a dishwasher • envelopes • a file • a freezer • a jacket
a jumper • kitchen roll • a lamp • melon • a notebook
oranges • a sofa • peaches • pens • postcards • salt
shampoo • sugar • a suit • washing powder • writing paper

CLOTHES	FURNITURE	ELECTRICAL APPLIANCES	HOUSEHOLD GOODS	STATIONERY	FRUIT

c. How many compound words or phrases can you make with the words *shop* or *shopping*? Write the exact words next to what they mean. One has been done for you.

1. _____*shop assistant*_____   person who works in a shop

2. _____   looking around the shop but not buying anything

3. _____   a list of things to buy

Shopping

4. _____ the window at the front of the shop

5. _____ an area with many shops, outside or indoors

6. _____ person who steals things from a shop

7. _____ a bag for carrying your shopping in

d. You might see these notices in a department store. Match them with their explanations.

CHANGING ROOMS NEXT TO LIFT
You may take in no more than
4 pieces of clothing

A

SORRY!
Lift to
childrenswear
**OUT OF
ORDER –**
Use escalator
in furniture
department

B

DO NOT
touch china!
Ask a shop
assistant to
serve you.

C

SPECIAL OFFER
ONLY FOR TODAY!
Prices on all sportswear
50% down

D

1. Because the lift is not working, you'll have to go upstairs another way

2. If you want to have a closer look at a porcelain teapot, try to find a shop assistant.

3. If you buy a tracksuit today you'll pay half its price.

4. There's a limit to the number of clothes you can try on each time.

e. Complete these three conversations at a market. Use the words in the box.

The oval ones, I think • They're £5 each. Crystal • Yes, here you are
Hello. Can I help you? • All right, £25 then
No, that's too big, do you have anything smaller? • What a pity, thanks anyway.

A   A Can I see that kitchen clock, please?

B   (1) _____

A   How much is it?

B   *£30.*

A   Oh no, that's too expensive.

B   (2) _____

B.   A How much are these wine glasses?

B   (3) _____

A   OK I'll take them.

B   *Which shape do you want? Round or oval?*

A   (4) _____

B   *Here you are. That's £10, please.*

A (5) _____

B   *Yes. What size is that coat?*

A   It's size 40.

B   (6) _____

A   No, I'm afraid this is the only one left.

B   (7) _____

f. Answer these questions about your shopping habits. Then ask one or two friends.

1.   How often do you go shopping? _____
_____

2.   Which kind of shopping do you dislike? _____
_____

3.   Do you prefer to shop in a big department store or a small shop? _____
_____

4.   How much do you spend on clothes per month? _____
_____

5.   What sort of things do you spend most of your money on? _____
_____

6.   Do you ever go shopping in an open market? _____
_____

7.   What do you think of on-line shopping? Have you ever bought anything over the Internet?
_____
_____

8.   Do you ever buy second-hand clothes? _____
_____

Signs & notices

a. Signs and notices often give you information (e.g. that an office is closed) or give you instructions (e.g. that you must keep quiet). Look at the notices below and decide whether they give you information or instructions.

1. THANK YOU FOR NOT SMOKING _____

2. OUT OF ORDER _____

3. NO PARKING _____

4. Do not leave your luggage unattended _____

5. EXIT staff only _____

6. SILENCE _____

7. NO CYCLING
   DOGS MUST BE ON LEAD _____

8. PAY HERE
   exact fare please
   NO NOTES _____

9. MESSAGE: Tanya – Greek class is on Tuesday afternoon this
   week instead of Monday, starting 20 minutes earlier than usual. _____

10. QUEUE THIS SIDE _____

11. Please ring for attention _____

12. SALE 30% OFF ALL ITEMS _____

b. Look at the signs in part a. again. Where would you see them? Choose from the list. You can use more than one answer.

1. airport _____

2. bus _____

3. cinema _____

4. clothes shop _____

5. hotel reception _____

6. hotel room door _____

7. library _____

8. post-it on someone's desk _____

9. public park _____

10. public phone _____

11. restaurant _____

12. street _____

c. The following words in the box usually appear in signs and public notices. Choose the correct word for each gap in the sentences below. You can only use each word/phrase once.

allowed	• area	• cancelled	• card	• changing rooms	• disabled
entrance	• forbidden	• hour	• instructions	• luggage	• may
no longer	• on time	• passengers	• property	• put	• responsible
	rooms	• seat	• use	• warning		

1. Do not _____ equipment in this box before reading _____.

2. Weekday parking: _____ than 20 minutes in any _____.

3. _____ coins in the coffee machine slowly – if in difficulty, go to room 2.

4. Smoking is _____ during lectures but is _____ during the coffee break.

5. This _____ is closed today – use back of building beside car park.

6. _____ for international flights – check in _____ here.

7. Visitors to the port _____ must collect an identity _____ at the main gate.

8. Offer this _____ to old or _____ people, or those carrying young children.

9. _____ next to escalator. Customers _____ take in no more than 4 pieces of clothing.

10. All the trains are running _____ today except the 8.15 which has been _____.

11. The College is not _____ for private _____ left in this building.

12. _____ – security cameras in use around this building.

---

d. Language focus

You may see the verbs *may, must* and *should* in signs and notices. Often these verbs do not appear in the signs but they help you to understand what the signs mean. It is important to understand the different meanings of these verbs.

e.g. **LEAVE LUGGAGE BESIDE RECEPTION AREA means**

You *may* leave your luggage beside the reception area OR You *are allowed to* leave your luggage beside the reception area.

PAY HERE means

You *must* pay here OR *It is necessary* that you pay here.

DRY CLEAN ONLY means

You *should* not wash this item of clothing OR *It is a good idea* not to wash this item of clothing.

Signs & notices

e. Do you understand the meaning of the signs below?

Use may, must, mustn't, should or shouldn't to complete the sentences under each sign so that they mean the same as the signs before them.

e.g.   PLEASE KNOCK BEFORE ENTERING

You should knock before you go in.

---

a.   DO NOT WALK ON THE GRASS

You _____ on the grass.

b.   BREAKFAST IS SERVED 7.00 TO 10.00

You _____ between 7 and 10 o'clock.

c.   KEEP MEDICINE OUT OF THE REACH OF CHILDREN

You _____ medicine near children.

d.   SLOW – CHILDREN PLAYING

You _____ slowly. There are children playing here.

e.   DO NOT LEAVE YOUR LUGGAGE UNATTENDED

You _____ luggage with you.

f.   QUEUE HERE TO BOOK TICKETS IN ADVANCE

You _____ if you want to book tickets in advance

g.   SAVER TICKETS CAN BE USED ON THE 9.30 TRAIN

You _____ saver tickets if you are on the 9.30 train.

h.   NO DIVING ALLOWED EXCEPT AT THE DEEP END OF THE SWIMMING POOL

You _____ if you are not at the deep end of the pool.

---

f. Can you find examples of signs or notices in English in your country? Where?

_____

_____

_____

_____

_____

_____

_____

78

a. Label the pictures with the names of sports and games in the box. You will only use 10 of them.

athletics • baseball • basketball • climbing • cricket • cycling
football • golf • hockey • ice skating • rugby • skiing
swimming • table tennis • tennis

1_____

2. _____

3._____

4. _____

5. _____

6. _____

7. _____

8. _____

9. _____

10. _____

b. Write down all the ball games from the box above. _____

_____

c. Which of the sports from above can you enjoy doing alone and not with other people? _____

_____

d. Which would you enjoy doing in your free time and which would you prefer to watch? _____

_____

e. Put these words into the correct columns.

ball • baseball • basket • boxing • car racing • court • crash helmet
field • gloves • golf clubs • net • pitch • pool • racket • shorts • skis
slope • stadium • swimming • track • trunks • whistle

Name of Sport	Place	Equipment

Sport

f. Match the sports on the left with the descriptions on the right.

1. Athletics •	• a.	You hit a ball with a club. You try to hit it into the hole
2. Basketball •	• b.	You hit the ball with a racket. You try to hit it over the net.
3. Golf •	• c.	You run round a track. The fastest wins the race.
4. Motor racing •	• d.	You ride round a track. The fastest horse wins the race.
5. Horse racing •	• e.	You drive round a track. The fastest wins a race.
6. Tennis •	• f.	You try to throw the ball into the basket.

g. Complete the sentences with the right form of the verbs _go_, _play_ or _do_.

1. In the summer I _____ a lot of water skiing. In the winter I _____ jogging every morning.

2. She doesn't _____ tennis very well because she doesn't _____ enough practice.

3. I can't _____ swimming today because I'm _____ volleyball in an hour with my team.

4. He _____ football with his friends on Sundays but he has no time to _____ any other sports. He's planning to _____ sailing next weekend.

h. Choose four sports that you have done and say if you enjoyed them and what it was like.
Then choose four that you haven't done but you would like to try and explain why.
Use these phrases.

I found _____ boring/exciting/frightening

I would find _____ difficult/easy/interesting

I was(n't) good at/bad at _____

I would(n't) be _____

i. Try to do this sports quiz with a friend. Don't worry if you cannot answer all the questions. But if you do you must be a sports expert!

1. Which is not an Olympic sport?
   a. judo b. tennis c. skateboarding d. football

2. Which country won the last World Cup of the 20th century?
   a. England b. Germany c. Brazil d. France

3. How many players are there in a volleyball team?
   a. nine b. six c. five d. eleven

4. Which footballer has married one of the Spice Girls?
   a. Diego Maradona b. Zinedine Zidane c. Ronaldo d. David Beckham

5. The first modern Olympic Games took place in _____
   a. Athens b. Berlin c. Rome d. London

6. A marathon runner has to run for just over _____ to finish the race.
   a. 20 km b. 30 km c. 40 km d. 50 km

7. Which American athlete won nine gold medals at four Olympic Games?
   a. Steffi Graf b. Carl Lewis c. Olga Korbut d. Muhammad Ali

Transport & travel

a. Put in the words below into the correct column. Each column describes a different means of transport. Some of the words can go into more then one column.

airport • bus stop • cab • carriage • coach • crossroads
driver • ferry • flight attendant • harbour • helicopter
junction • motorway • pilot • platform • railway • runway
station • taxi • terminal • traffic lights

BUS	AIR	TRAIN	CAR	SEA

b. Match the verbs on the left with the nouns on the right to describe ways of travelling.

1. get in/out of the   •   •   a. bicycle, boat, bus, car, coach, ferry, plane, train
2. get on/off the   •   •   b. bus, car, coach, lorry
3. go by   •   •   c. bike, horse, motorbike, motorcycle
4. go on the   •   •   d. car
5. ride a   •   •   e. bicycle, boat, bus, coach, ferry, plane, train
6. drive a   •   •   f. bus, coach, ferry, underground, train

c. The adjectives in the box can be used to describe public transport. Use some of them to fill the gaps in the sentences below.

cheap • comfortable • crowded • empty • expensive • fast
reliable • safe • slow • uncomfortable

1. This train is too _____. It stops at every little station on the way.

2. The train journey was long and _____. The seats were so hard.

3. The underground is always _____ during the rush hour. You can never find a seat.

4. Taxi fares to the airport are very _____. You may have to pay more than £30!

5. Going by coach is fairly _____. Most people can afford the fare.

Transport & travel

d. All the words in the box are about *air travel*. Put them into the right column. There may be more than one correct answer.

> air terminal • cabin crew • check-in desk • customs • departure lounge
> duty free • excess baggage • landing • pilot • runway • seat belt
> take-off • upright position

DEPARTURES	THE FLIGHT	ARRIVAL

e. Now match five of the words above with their definitions below

1. The money you have to pay if your luggage is too heavy _____

2. The people who look after you on the plane _____

3. The part of the airport you walk through when you arrive or depart _____

4. The place you go when you arrive at the airport with your luggage _____

5. The correct way to have your seat during landing and take-off _____

f. Fill in the gaps in the text below with A, B, C or D.

Heathrow Airport is (0) ___*C*___ of the busiest (1) _____ airports in the world. More than 90 (2) _____ use Heathrow to fly direct to about 200 (3) _____ in 85 countries in the world. Every year Heathrow handles 450,000 international (4) _____, an average of 1300 per day. This is more than one a minute from six o'clock in the morning till midnight. Almost 58,000 people (5) _____ at Heathrow, that's the population of a small town. There are around 75,000,000 (6) _____ of baggage going through Heathrow each year and there are over 9,500 baggage (7) _____ available for passengers – more than in any other airport. Passengers (8) _____ 26,000 cups of tea and 6,500 sandwiches at Heathrow every day and the duty-free (9) _____ sell a bottle of whisky every 7 seconds – that's more than 500 bottles an hour. The most common illness among passengers is heart attack. Around 40 people every year die in this way while (10) _____ to or through Heathrow.

0. A. an	B. some	C. one	D. all
1. A. local	B. international	C. famous	D. public
2. A. planes	B. tourists	C. airlines	D. airports
3. A. destinations	B. countries	C. terminals	D. runways
4. A. trips	B. journeys	C. airplanes	D. flights
5. A. fly	B. work	C. travel	D. board
6. A. suitcases	B. bags	C. bits	D. pieces
7. A. buses	B. baskets	C. collectors	D. trolleys
8. A. drink	B. eat	C. buy	D. sell
9. A. shops	B. points	C. corners	D. trolleys
10. A. arriving	B. travelling	C. landing	D. commuting

a. Complete the table with the missing adjectives or nouns.

NOUN	ADJECTIVE	NOUN	ADJECTIVE
1. sun	_____	6. shower	_____
2. _____	icy	7. _____	humid
3. fog	_____	8. cloud	_____
4. mist	_____	9. wind	_____
5. _____	climatic	10. _____	hot

b. Match the weather symbols with the right words. You won't use all of them.

clear • cloudy • drizzle • fog • freezing • frosty • rain • hot • ice
mist • rainy • showers • snow • sunny • temperatures below zero
thunderstorms • wet • windy • wind speed and direction

1._____   2._____   3._____   4._____   5._____   6._____   7._____

c. Are these sentences true or false? If you think a sentence is false write the true sentence. Use your dictionary to make sure.

1. A shower is a light wind. _____

2. It often pours with rain in the desert. _____

3. You always enjoy a cool breeze on a very hot day. _____

4. It usually gets frosty in very high temperatures. _____

5. When it's very foggy a flight may be delayed. _____

6. If it is humid the air will be very dry. _____

7. Water can turn into ice if the temperature is below zero. _____

8. Lightning is a loud noise in the air followed by thunder. _____

9. It can get quite chilly in the desert in the evening. _____

10. Temperatures below zero are very unusual in the mountains in Switzerland. _____

Weather

d. Match the beginnings with the right endings to make logical sentences.

1. It was getting dark •	•	a. so I decided not to drive.
2. It was pouring with rain •	•	b. so he put on his sunglasses.
3. It was getting very hot •	•	c. so we had dinner on the balcony.
4. It was extremely icy •	•	d. so we had our picnic indoors.
5. It was very windy •	•	e. so they had to drink a lot of water.
6. It was too bright •	•	f. so the ferry didn't go.
7. It was freezing •	•	g. so I put on a thick coat and gloves.
8. It was nice and warm •	•	h. so we lit a fire.

e. Read the text and fill the gaps with A, B or C.

The weather (1) _____ for noon tomorrow:

Temperatures will be generally (2) _____ in Scotland and the north of England, but will be (3) _____ zero in the rest of the country. There will be (4)_____ rain in Scotland, moving into northern England later in the afternoon. Wales and the South West will be cloudy with (5) _____ intervals and with (6) _____ of up to 15 miles an hour. The South East will be (7) _____ and foggy but it will become (8) _____ and dry later. The rest of England will be cloudy with a few (9) _____ and even some snow in inland areas. In Northern Ireland, (10) _____ will be just above zero.

1. A. news	B. preview	C. forecast
2. A. big	B. high	C. above
3. A. more	B. under	C. below
4. A. heavy	B. strong	C. much
5. A. warm	B. sunny	C. clear
6. A. temperatures	B. rain	C. winds
7. A. sunny	B. wet	C. drizzle
8. A. clear	B. rainy	C. damp
9. A. showers	B. intervals	C. rain
10. A. winds	B. temperatures	C. thunderstorms

f. Match the word clouds with the texts below. Then fill the gaps choosing words from the right cloud.

below –20°C / little rain hot and dry / snow

very humid / 24 and 27°C wet season / tropical

not too cold – sunshine fresh breeze / hot and dry

A. In Russia the weather is mainly _____ in the summers with temperatures of 25–30°C. Winters are freezing cold and it snows a lot. Temperatures can drop _____ and there is often _____ from November to March. Spring comes late in Moscow and it is normally quite warm and bright. There is very_____.

B. In Kenya the climate is _____. It is very hot all year round and the temperature is between _____ and is the same in July and January. From November to April is the _____ and in January it rains a lot. From July to September it is mostly dry but the air is _____.

C. In Greece summers are usually very _____ with a temperature of 30° to 35°C. On the islands it is always a little cooler with a nice _____ and lots of _____. Sometimes it gets very windy. Winters are _____ but it usually rains in October and November. Sometimes there is snow mainly in the mountains.

g. What's the weather like in your country or your town? Write a letter to an English-speaking friend and describe the weather in your country for all the year round.

Work & jobs

a. All the words in the box describe different jobs. Put them into the right column. Some words may fit in more than one category.

builder • dentist • doctor • dustman • editor • fire fighter
journalist • lecturer • newscaster • nurse • plumber • police officer
professor • psychologist • publisher • reporter • social worker
surgeon • taxi driver • teacher • traffic warden • tutor • writer

EDUCATION	HEALTH	PUBLIC SERVICES	MANUAL JOBS	MEDIA

b. Match the jobs on the left with the subjects on the right.

Profession		Subject studied
1. lawyer	•	• a. cookery
2. tourist guide	•	• b. accountancy
3. chemist	•	• c. law
4. musician	•	• d. architecture
5. doctor	•	• e. acting
6. journalist	•	• f. tourism
7. physicist	•	• g. physics
8. sales and marketing manager	•	• h. chemistry
9. accountant	•	• i. medicine
10. chef	•	• j. journalism
11. actor/actress	•	• k. music
12. architect	•	• l. marketing

Work & jobs

c. Complete the table below with the missing words or phrases. One has been done for you.

JOB	PLACE	DUTIES
pilot	*aeroplane*	*flies a plane*
	library	
		writes newspaper reports
secretary		
vet		
		teaches History
	university	
		fixes water pipes
hairdresser		
	police station	

d. This is what happened to Malcolm with his last job. Can you put the events in the right order?

1. He applied for the job. _____

2. He got promotion. _____

3. They weren't pleased with his work. _____

4. He accepted the job. _____

5. He saw the advertisement. _____

6. They sacked him. _____

7. They offered him the job. _____

8. They gave him an interview. _____

e. Match the verbs on the left with the nouns/phrases on the right to make the right expressions.

1.	attend	•	• a.	job satisfaction
2.	deal with	•	• b.	overtime
3.	do	•	• c.	the accounts department
4.	earn	•	• d.	customers
5.	get	•	• e.	£350 per hour
6.	meet	•	• f.	meetings
7.	run	•	• g.	a lot of paperwork
8.	work	•	• h.	customers' complaints

f. Complete each second sentence so that it means the same as the first one. Use the words in bold and make any necessary changes.

1. He is responsible for the production department.   **charge**

   He is _____ of the production department.

2. In my job I have to visit clients at their workplace.   **involves**

   My job _____ clients at their workplace.

3. She retired early and went to live on an island.   **retirement**

   She took _____ and went to live on an island.

4. I earn £25,000 a year.   **salary**

   My _____ £25,000 a year.

5. She would prefer a job with regular working hours.   **nine-to-five**

   She would prefer a _____ job.

6. He gets £25,000 from his teaching job and another £10,000 from writing.   **income**

   His total _____ £35,000.

g. Use 1 to 10 (1= best, 10=worst) to put the jobs listed below in order of preference. Think in terms of a)*pay* and b)*job satisfaction*. Answer it for yourself first and then ask a friend.

JOBS	PAY	JOB SATISFACTION
Archaeologist		
Bank manager		
English teacher		
Journalist		
Nurse		
Police officer		
Professional footballer		
Secretary		
Shop assistant		
TV presenter		
IT specialist		
Artist		

Phonetic symbols

It is not always easy to pronounce words in English because very often words are not written the way they are pronounced. The phonetic symbols after each word in your dictionary show you how to say each word.

> telephone   [ˈtelɪfəʊn] **1** *noun* machine which you use to speak to someone who is some distance away; *can't someone answer the telephone – it's been ringing and ringing; she lifted the telephone and called the ambulance* **2** *verb* to call someone using a telephone; *your sister telephoned when you were out*

There is an explanation of the phonetic symbols used throughout your dictionary together with examples at the starting pages.

Some of the phonetic symbols are pronounced in the same way as the letter they look like, e.g. /p/ sounds like 'p' in 'pet'. But all the others change their pronunciation according to the word they are in. This is why it is important you familiarise yourself with the phonetic symbols in your dictionary.

a. Use phonetic symbols to fill in the pronunciation of the following words. Write the phonetic symbols between the / /. Also practise saying them.

1. back: /   / bacon: /   /   4. curry: /   / curtain: /   /
2. cough: /   / enough: /   /   5. now: /   / know: /   /
3. vase: /   / razor: /   /   6. through: /   / throw: /   /

b. Match these words with their pronunciation.

1. chilly	•	•	a. /rʌf/
2. cinema	•	•	b. /tuː/
3. deal	•	•	c. /tɪər/
4. dial	•	•	d. /miːl/
5. feel	•	•	e. /ˈsɪnəmə/
6. fill	•	•	f. /ˈtʃɪlɪ/
7. meal	•	•	g. /fiːl/
8. rough	•	•	h. /diːl/
9. two	•	•	i. /ˈdaɪəl/
10. tear	•	•	j. /fɪl/

c. All the following words describe colours. Match them with their phonetic symbols.

1. orange	•	•	/bluːˈ
2. white	•	•	/griːn/
3. beige	•	•	/pɪŋk/
4. yellow	•	•	/greɪ/
5. brown	•	•	/ˈɑrɪndʒ/
6. grey	•	•	/ˈpəːpl/
7. pink	•	•	/beɪʒ/
8. purple	•	•	/waɪt/
9. green	•	•	/ˈjeləʊ/
10. blue	•	•	/braun/

d. Underline the silent letter in each of these words.

1. island
2. know
3. wrist
4. hour
5. two
6. knock
7. while

e. Use your dictionary to find out which of the four words on the right is the odd one out because it does not rhyme with the word on the left.

1.	heard	word	bird	beard	third
2.	dead	bed	bead	said	thread
3.	meat	seat	suite	threat	treat
4.	bear	pear	there	fear	stare
5.	steak	beak	bake	break	stake
6.	worse	purse	nurse	horse	hearse
7.	weight	wait	hate	straight	height
8.	thumb	come	sum	home	some
9.	trouble	cousin	rough	wound	tough
10.	sew	few	so	low	show
11.	shown	phone	town	loan	tone
12.	fear	beer	dear	leer	bear
13.	should	mould	could	wood	good
14.	please	freeze	cheese	peace	tease
15.	paid	afraid	made	weighed	said
16.	soul	goal	hole	whole	foul
17.	tool	pool	wool	cool	fool
18.	won	son	sun	one	gone
19.	catch	match	latch	batch	watch
20.	loose	choose	moose	juice	sluice
21.	wonder	blunder	thunder	wander	plunder
22.	walk	work	talk	pork	cork
23.	fruit	shoot	loot	boot	foot
24.	chase	vase	face	lace	race

Punctuation & spelling

We use punctuation in writing in order to show when we finish or start a sentence, if a word is a capital name or not. There are certain symbols, called punctuation marks e.g. comma, full stop, exclamation mark, etc. There are some basic rules about how to use punctuation marks.

a. Match the punctuation marks with their names and their use.

1.	!	a.	question mark	I.	at the end of a sentence
2.	""	b.	colon	II.	to separate two parts of a sentence
3.	( )	c.	hyphen	III.	for missing letters / for possessives
4.	,	d.	exclamation mark	IV.	to separate extra information from the sentence
5.	–	e.	period or full stop	V.	after a direct question
6.	:	f.	quotation marks	VI.	for a pause in a long sentence
7.	;	g.	dash	VII.	to join two words together
8.	?	h.	apostrophe	VIII.	at the end of a sentence to express surprise
9.	.	i.	brackets	IX.	to introduce a list or a quotation in a sentence
10.	-	j.	semi-colon	X.	to separate parts of sentences
11.	'	k.	comma	XI.	to show that words are spoken

b. Use the right punctuation marks in the following sentences.

1. What an amazing story

2. I ran all the way to the station but I still missed the train

3. Come and see whats happened said John

4. I spoke to David yesterday he can't come to the meeting tonight

5. Whats your passport number the policeman asked

6. I need some butter eggs yoghurt and sugar

7. I dont know whos ordered this but it wasnt me said the old man

8. The car the one with the broken window was parked outside our house

c. It is important to know the English alphabet and the order of the letters. Very often you have to spell your name, the name of another person or the name of a place.

Also in your dictionary you will find the words explained in alphabetical order.

All the words in the box are sports. Write them in alphabetical order.

swimming	• golf	• tennis	• cycling	• basketball	• skiing
	rugby	• cricket	• football	• boxing	

1. _____   3. _____   5. _____   7. _____   9. _____

2. _____   4. _____   6. _____   8. _____   10. _____

Punctuation & spelling

d. Now write these words in alphabetical order as quickly as you can

wild • white • wheel • wheat • weight • whale • why • which

1. _____

2. _____

3. _____

4. _____

5. _____

6. _____

7. _____

8. _____

e. Spell the names of the following cities for a friend.

1. Moscow
2. Tokyo
3. Singapore
4. Marseilles
5. Athens
6. Rio de Janeiro

f. Many words in English have irregular plural forms. Write the plural of these nouns.

1. house _____ 2. match _____ 3. fax _____

4. loss _____ 5. baby _____ 6. university _____

g. Some words in English have the same or very similar sounds but they are spelled differently. Choose the correct word to complete these sentences.

1. Oh *dear / deer*! I've lost my pen!

2. She had to *brake / break* hard as the car in front stopped without a warning.

3. I bought this crystal vase for £15 in a *sale / sail*.

4. Stir the *flour / flower* into the cake mixture.

5. Please keep *quiet / quite*! I'm trying to work.

6. 'Cinderella' used to be my favourite fairy *tale / tail* when I was a child.

7. We had a *grate / great* time at the party last night.

8. She measures 80cm around the *waist / waste*.

9. Let me *sow / sew* this tear in your shirt.

10. He asked his secretary to bring the *mail / male*.

91

Word stress & pronunciation

When a word has two or more syllables, one of them has the main stress. This means that this syllable is said louder than the others. In English It is very important to put the stress on the right part of the word, otherwise it can be difficult for others to understand what you are saying.

In your dictionary the symbol (') shows you where the main stress of each word is. But this is only a guide because the stress of each word can change according to the word's position in the sentence.

Sometimes when you use a different form of a word you should change the position of the main stress of the word. This can also change the pronunciation of the word.

Look up these words in your dictionary and notice how, as the stress changes, so does the pronunciation of the vowels.

*ph*otograph
phot*o*graphy
photo*gra*phic

Some words can be both nouns and verbs without changing their form. Nouns often have the stress on their first syllable. Verbs often have the stress on their second syllable. Sometimes the pronunciation changes too.

Look up these words in your dictionary. Does the pronunciation of the vowels change together with the stress?

record (noun)   record (verb)

produce (noun)   produce (verb)

increase (noun)   increase (verb)

a. Look at the words below. Which ones have the stress on the first syllable?

1. amused
2. annoyed
3. astonished
4. depressed
5. excited
6. grateful
7. happy
8. jealous
9. impatient
10. miserable
11. thoughtful
12. worried

b. Underline the part of each word that has the main stress.

1. father
2. education
3. necessary
4. fortunately
5. advertisement
6. organise
7. dangerous

8. wonderful

9. computer

10. photographer

11. anxious

12 below

13. preferred

14. expected

15. police

c. Choose the correctly stressed words below. Use your dictionary.

1. Did you **re**cord / re**cord** the film on video?

2. There has been a 10% **in**crease / in**crease** of the price of petrol this month.

3. She was let out of prison for good **con**duct / con**duct**.

4. The regulations do not **per**mit / per**mit** smoking inside the building.

5. Have you bought her a **pre**sent / pre**sent** for her birthday?

6. Air pollution will **in**crease / in**crease** in the next few years.

7. She is going to **pre**sent / pre**sent** the campaign plan to the board directors.

8. He has broken the world **re**cord / re**cord** twice.

9. Do I need a **per**mit / per**mit** to work abroad?

10. He is going to **con**duct / con**duct** the orchestra at the Festival Hall tonight.

d. Look up these word groups in your dictionary to find out if the main stress changes position according to the word form

1. employ – employee

2. present (n) – present (v)

3. answer (n) – answer (v)

4. advertise – advertisement

5. disagree – disagreement

6. depart – departure

7. discuss – discussion

8. operate – operator – operation

9. suspect (n) – suspect (v)

10. origin – original

93

Vocabulary record sheet

TOPIC:

WORD OR EXPRESSION	DEFINITION	SAMPLE SENTENCE(S)
shop assistant	*a person who works in a shop*	*The shop assistant offered to help me ..*

Vocabulary record sheet

WORD OR EXPRESSION	DEFINITION	SAMPLE SENTENCE(S)

Vocabulary record sheet

WORD OR EXPRESSION	DEFINITION	SAMPLE SENTENCE(S)

Vocabulary record sheet

WORD OR EXPRESSION	DEFINITION	SAMPLE SENTENCE(S)

Phrasal verbs record sheet

MAIN VERB: look

PHRASAL VERB	DEFINITION	SAMPLE SENTENCE(S)
look after	*take care of*	*Will you look after the plants for me*

Phrasal verbs record sheet

PHRASAL VERB	DEFINITION	SAMPLE SENTENCE(S)

Phrasal verbs record sheet

PHRASAL VERB	DEFINITION	SAMPLE SENTENCE(S)

Word forms record sheet

Photocopy and use this sheet to keep a record of different word forms. You will not need to use all of the spaces on the sheet. Two examples have been given.

VERB 1	VERB 2	ADJECTIVE 1	ADJECTIVE 2	NOUN 1	NOUN 2
agree	disagree	agreeable	disagreeable	agreement	disagreement
_____	_____	happy	unhappy	happiness	unhappiness

Word forms record sheet

VERB 1	VERB 2	ADJECTIVE 1	ADJECTIVE 2	NOUN 1	NOUN 2

Word forms record sheet

VERB 1	VERB 2	ADJECTIVE 1	ADJECTIVE 2	NOUN 1	NOUN 2

Answer key

SECTION 2: WORDS & GRAMMAR

Adjectives (pp. 1–2)

a.
GOOD: amazing, brilliant, fantastic, fascinating, fine, great, happy, interesting, kind, lovely, perfect, super
BAD: boring, difficult, horrible, nasty, naughty

b.

1	d	6.	e
2.	h	7.	a
3.	c	8.	k
4.	b	9.	f
5.	g		

c. (suggested answers)
1. good, great, lovely, fantastic, etc.
2. miserable, difficult, boring
3. kind, nice
4. heavy
5. excellent, wonderful, fantastic, good, etc.
6. naughty
7. wonderful, lovely, etc.
8. outrageous, horrible, awful, etc.
9. nasty, bad, awful, etc.
10. excellent, great, etc.
11. amazing, fascinating, exciting, terrific, etc.
12. brilliant, fantastic, gorgeous, dreadful, etc.

d.
1. surprised
2. embarrassing
3. frightened
4. annoying
5. excited

e.
1. . . . frightening for most students
2. . . . bored at the meeting . . .
3. . . . disappointed . . .
4. . . . confusing (for me) . . .

Adverbs (pp. 3–5)

a.
hardly ever = rarely or never, normally = regularly, not very often = rarely,
now and then = occasionally or sometimes, often = frequently, seldom = rarely, usually = regularly

b.
1. usually, often
2. rarely
3. always, normally
4. always, normally
5. never
6. frequently, often

c. (open answers)

d.
1 very
2. pretty, very, rather
3. extremely
4. rather, quite
5. pretty, rather, quite
6. a bit

e.
1. quietly
2. careful
3. fast
4. badly
5. polite
6. awfully
7. angry
8. hard

f.
1. well
2. good
3. well
4. good
5. well; good
6. well

g.
1. angrily
2. slowly
3. firmly
4. carefully
5. directly
6. properly
7. immediately
8. strongly
9. safely
10. usually
11. patiently
12. probably

Comparatives & superlatives (pp. 6–8)

a.
angry – angrier – angriest
beautiful – more beautiful – most beautiful,
boring – more boring – most boring,
cheap – cheaper – cheapest
clear – clearer – clearest
cold – colder – coldest
comfortable – more comfortable – most comfortable
crazy – crazier – craziest
difficult – more difficult – most difficult
dirty – dirtier – dirtiest
energetic – more energetic – most energetic,
filthy – filthier – filthiest
frightening – more frightening – most frightening
high – higher – highest
long – longer – longest
nice – nicer – nicest
noisy – noisier – noisiest
safe – safer – safest
serious – more serious – most serious
unhappy – more unhappy – most unhappy

b.
1. warmer
2. more crowded
3. worst
4. fastest
5. bigger
6. more interesting
7. most delicious
8. richest
9. happier
10. simpler

c.
1. . . . is worse . . .
2. . . . are faster than . . .
3. *correct*
4. . . . bed earlier than . . .
5. . . . a better player . . .
6. . . . is more modern than . . .
7. . . . .is as old as . . .
8. *correct*
9. . . . is friendlier than . . .
10. . . . not as difficult as . . .

d.
1. later, earlier
2. oldest, most expensive, smallest
3. most luxurious, newest, most expensive, cheapest
4. older

Compound nouns (pp. 9–11)

a. (See your dictionary)

b. Things we wear: earrings, raincoat, sunglasses, swimming costume

People: babysitter, bodyguard, boyfriend, grandchildren

Roads: car park, parking meter, pedestrian crossing, traffic lights

Money: bank account, cash desk, cheque book, income tax

c.

1.	income tax	9.	grandchildren
2.	babysitter	10.	raincoat
3.	sunglasses	11.	earrings
4.	car park	12.	bodyguards
5.	bank account	13.	parking meter
6.	swimming costume	14.	pedestrian crossing
7.	traffic lights	15.	boyfriend
8.	cash desk	16.	chequebook

d. (suggested answers)

birthday card, booking office, boyfriend, traffic lights, sunset, frying pan, living room

e. (open answers)

Conjunctions & connectives (pp. 12–14)

Conjunction	Function
and	tells you more
but	makes a contrast
so	tells you the result
or	gives you a choice
when	answers the question *'when?'*
although	tells you something surprising
if	makes a condition
after, before	answers the question *'what happened first?'*
because	answers the question *'why?'*

Connecting word	Function
only	says that something is not very big or not very much
like	makes a comparison
than	is used after a comparative adjective or adverb
even	says something is surprising or unusual
too, as well, also	says something is extra

a.

b.

1.	and	6.	as well
2.	but	7.	because
3.	or	8.	although
4.	so	9.	than
5.	only	10.	if

c.

1. Although I didn't know many people
2. . . . because she had studied very hard
3. . . . if you don't listen carefully
4. . . . although we live in the same street
5. . . . after he had worked/working in a bookshop for two years
6. . . . before/until the lights went green
7. . . . if you speak more slowly
8. . . . because I had an umbrella

d.

1.	too/as well	5.	than
2.	Even	6.	also
3.	like	7.	too/as well
4.	Only		

e. (suggested answers)

1. . . . it helps me to remember their meaning.
2. . . . you are learning English.
3. . . . you visit England.
4. . . . you take an exam.
5. . . . you can practise listening to English on your own.
6. . . . they understand most of what they read or hear.

f.

1.	b)	6.	d)
2.	c)	7.	a)
3.	a)	8.	c)
4.	d)	9.	b)
5.	b)	10.	c)

Countable/uncountable nouns (pp. 15–17)

a.

1.	C, U	9.	C, U
2.	U, C	10.	C, U
3.	U	11.	U, C
4.	U	12.	C, C
5.	C, U	13.	U, U
6.	U	14.	C
7.	U, C	15.	U, C
8.	C, U		

b.

1 . . . . some information about . . .
2. . . . usually better weather . . .
3. *correct*
4. . . . very good advice.
5. . . . .in the house is very old.
6. . . . making progress with . . .
7. *correct*
8. find new accommodation
9. . . . .a lot of housework . . .
10. *correct*
11. . . . carried my luggage to . . .
12. I'd like fish and chips . . .

c.

1.	a	6.	many, a/the
2.	*blank*	7.	an, *blank*
3.	much	8.	much
4.	*blank*, much	9.	many
5.	the, *blank*	10.	*blank*, a

Answer key

d.

1. transport
2. accommodation
3. news
4. information
5. furniture
6. countryside, scenery
7. money
8. traffic

e.

1. . . . is central heating in my flat
2. . . are job advertisements . . .
3. . . . .English is . . .
4. It's a . . . . . .
5. . . . .was no more room . . .
6. . . . news I had today is . . .

Prefixes (pp. 18–19)

a. (suggested answers)

il – used before words beginning with *l*
ir – used before words beginning with *r*
im – used before words beginning with *p*
un– used before many different words

b.

disagree
unemployed
invisible
unlock
illegal
irregular
informal
dishonest
undressed
unhappy
misunderstand
unlike/dislike

c.

1. . . . unemployed
2. . . . untidy
3. . . . impatient
4. . . . illegal
5. . . . misunderstood it
6. . . . invisible
7. . . . undressed

d.

1. g
2. e
3. b
4. d
5. c
6. a
7. f

e.

1. impossible
2. halfway
3. uncomfortable
4. disappear
5. ex-wife
6. misunderstood
7. reorganizing
8. unlock
9. unpacked

Prepositions (pp. 20–22)

a.

1. at
2. in
3. on
4. at
5. on, in
6. at
7. in, at
8. in
9. on
10. at

b.

1. in front of
2. over, below
3. above
4. behind
5. into
6. up

c.

1. in
2. *blank*
3. at/on
4. for
5. *blank*
6. *blank*
7. in
8. to
9. *blank*
10. for
11. with
12. after
13. *blank*
14. on
15. for

d.

1. B
2. C
3. D
4. B
5. A
6. B
7. B
8. D
9. B
10. C

e. (open answers)

Suffixes (pp. 23–24)

a.

1. e
2. f
3. b
4. g
5. a
6. c
7. i
8. d
9. j
10. h

b.

amusement, digestion, discussion, enjoyment, government, happiness, impression, information, invitation, measurement, popularity, preparation, protection, punishment, responsibility, revision, sadness, statement, suggestion, television

c.

1. discussion
2. television
3. revision
4. protection
5. information
6. suggestion
7. preparation
8 invitation

d.

1. singer
2. employer
3. farmer
4. dancer
5. director
6. artist
7. actor/actress
8. manager
9. driver
10. trainer

e. (suggested answers)

1. careless
2. hopeless
3. useless
4. painless
5. endless

f. (open answers)

Word partners (pp. 25–26)

a.

1. h
2. e
6. d
7. b

3.	a	8.	j
4.	f	9.	c
5.	g	10.	i

b.

1.	start	6.	run
2.	tell	7.	have/had
3.	do	8.	ask
4.	take	9.	make
5.	surfing	10.	get off

c.

strong tea, coffee, accent
heavy traffic, smoker, rain
hard examination, work, effort
dry weather, wine, cleaning
great success, actor, time

d.

1.	heavy	6.	strong
2.	strong	7.	hard
3.	heavy	8.	great
4.	dry	9.	dry
5.	great	10.	hard

e.

1.	highly	4.	awfully
2.	extremely	5.	completely
3.	absolutely	6.	really

f.

1.	out of work/without work	4.	by mistake
2.	by himself	5.	by chance
3.	on the phone	6.	at the moment

Words you may confuse (pp. 27–28)

a.

three meanings as a noun, one meaning as a verb, three meanings as an adjective

b.

1. noun – being bright
2. verb – make something start to burn
3. noun – electric bulb which gives light
4. adjective – not dark
5. noun – being bright
6. adjective – not heavy
7. noun – make something easier to understand
8. noun – electric bulb which gives light

c.

1.	quiet	4.	quite
2.	quite	5.	quite
3.	quiet		

d.

1. . . . .she made many mistakes
2. They made a lot. . . .
3. correct
4. . . . .having/taking an exam. . .
5. . . . take/make a decision. . .
6. . . . does her washing . . .
7. correct

8.	. . . take a taxi . . .		
9.	. . . is having a baby . . .		
10.	. . . .he do his homework . . .		

e.

1.	h	6.	c
2.	g	7.	d
3.	a	8.	f
4.	j	9.	e
5.	i	10.	b

f.

1.	lose	9.	expect
2.	fell	10.	robbed
3.	checked	11.	quite, felt
4.	cook	12.	made
5.	bring	13.	had
6.	lend	14.	break
7.	work	15.	remind
8.	taught		

SECTION 3: VERBS

Modal verbs (pp. 29–30)

a.

three meanings of *may*

b.

1. asking politely
2. it's possible
3. it is allowed
4. it's possible
5. perhaps
6. it's probable

c.

1.	e	5.	c
2.	g	6.	b
3.	h	7.	f
4.	a	8.	d

d. (suggested answers)

1.	should	6.	don't have to
2.	have to/must	7.	must
3.	should	8.	shouldn't
4.	may/might	9.	must/may
5.	shouldn't	10.	shouldn't/mustn't

e.

1. . . . .have to/must check in . . .
2. . . . mustn't smoke . . .
3. . . . have to/need to/must learn . . . .
4. .. . . should book . . .
5. . . . mustn't/cannot have . . .
6. . . . should ask for . . .
7. . . . don't need to/needn't/don't have to take . . .
8. . . . may use . . .
9. . . . must/have to show . . .
10. . . . must register . . .

f. (suggested answers)

1. You mustn't leave anything valuable in the van.
2. You should/must have the exact amount of money for your ticket.

Answer key

3. You must keep your dog on a lead.
4. You have to/must check the screens for flight information.
5. You have to/must take one tablet . . .

Phrasal verbs (pp. 31–32)

a. (open answers)

b.

1. doing/progressing
2. went inside
3. is not friendly with
4. getting older

c.

1.	out	6.	behind
2.	over	7.	with
3.	off	8.	off
4.	on	9.	off
5.	off	10.	for

d.

1.	look	11.	look
2.	take	12.	getting
3.	gone	13.	pick
4.	get	14.	keep/stay
5.	turn	15.	turn
6.	go	16.	keep
7.	run	17.	put
8.	give	18.	put
9.	went	19.	look
10.	going	20.	hurry

e.

1. . . . wake him up
2. . . . I'll tidy it up
3. . . . I'll switch/turn it off
4. . . . I'll turn it on
5. . . . I'll put it out
6. . . . I'll put/take it out
7. . . . I'll turn it down

f. (suggested answers)

1. . . . in London/Paris/Madrid
2. . . . the bank vault/car/house
3. . . . my car
4. . . . her shoes/coat
5. . . . the money she owed me
6. . . . how much you've grown!
7. . . . the money for the water bill
8. . . . the rubbish for collection tomorrow morning
9. . . . the train at his stop
10. . . . your raincoat, it looks wet outside

Verb forms & verb patterns (pp. 33–34)

a.

1.	c	4.	e
2.	d	5.	b
3.	f	6.	a

b.

1. I would like you to leave.
2. Can I apologise for my mistake?

3. Please explain to me what to do.
4. He suggested I (should) tell the police about it.
5. I insist (that) you come.
6. correct
7. We discussed my report . . .
8. correct
9. . . . persuade her to come . . .
10. Please tell her/him I am . . .

c. (suggested answers)

1. . . . turning the heating on
2. . . . it in class
3. . . . them to you
4. . . . her to lie down
5. . . . me how to get there

d.

1.	to study	6.	to help
2.	using	7.	working
3.	to finish	8.	driving
4.	living	9.	to let
5.	to pass	10.	to buy

e.

1.	to change	9.	to slow
2.	working	10.	driving
3.	to leave	11.	to see
4.	to become	12.	coming
5.	to tell	13.	to bring
6.	to drive	14.	to meet
7.	to let	15.	writing
8.	to learn	16.	seeing

SECTION 4: TOPICS

Animals & pets (pp. 35–36)

a. (suggested answers)

FARM ANIMALS: cow, donkey, goat, hen, horse, lamb, pig, sheep
WILD/ZOO ANIMALS: bear, camel, giraffe, lion, monkey, rabbit, snake, tortoise
INSECTS/BIRDS: ant, bee, budgie, butterfly, fly, mosquito, parrot, robin, spider
PETS: cat, dog, goldfish, hamster, horse, parrot, rabbit, tortoise

b. (suggested answers)

1.	Giraffes	5.	Sheep
2.	Dogs	6.	Bees
3.	Parrots	7.	Snakes
4.	Cows	8.	Lions

c.

cow – calf
hen – chick
goat – kid
pig – piglet
sheep – lamb

d.

0.	B	6.	C
1.	C	7.	B
2.	C	8.	C
3.	D	9.	A
4.	A	10.	D
5.	B		

e. (open answers)

British & American English (pp. 37–38)

a. (suggested answers)

British English: autumn, biscuits, car park, chips, lift, lorry, motorway, rubbish, sweets, toilet, trainers, trousers, vest, wardrobe

American English: apartment, cab, candy, closet, cookies, elevator, fall, French fries, garbage, highway, pants, parking lot, semester, subway, truck, vacation

b.

British English	American English
sweets	candy
fortnight	two weeks
chips	*French fries*
waistcoat	vest
petrol	*gas*
pavement	*sidewalk*
trainers	sneakers
football	*soccer*
crisps	*chips*

c.

1. color – US
2. traveler–US
3. dialog – US
4. center–US
5. meter – US
6. license – US
7. labor – US
8. canceling – US

d.

tomato, schedule, ballet, zebra

e.

British English
1. wardrobe
2. bin
3. biscuits
4. motorway
5. fortnight
6. rubber
7. term
8. underground
9. lift
10. sweets
11. timetable
12. waistcoat

American English
1. closet
2. trashcan
3. cookies
4. highway
5. two weeks
6. eraser
7. semester
8. subway
9. elevator
10. candy
11. schedule
12. vest

f.

It was a warm day in the autumn. I had been driving along the motorway since eight o'clock in the morning. Now it was getting near lunchtime and I needed to fill up the car and get something to eat. So I drove towards the nearest town, left the car in a car park by the main road and took a taxi to the centre. I started walking around and it was getting hot. Then I saw a nice little restaurant with tables out on the pavement. I had a hamburger with salad and chips and drank a cool beer. I started talking with a lorry driver who told me where to find a petrol station. I thanked him and looked for a phone box to call my wife. It was really a nice break.

Clothes (pp. 39–40)

a.

HEAD: cap, earrings, hat, scarf, sunglasses
CHEST: cardigan, jacket, jumper, shirt, sweater, T-shirt, tie, vest, waistcoat
LEGS: boots, jeans, shorts, skirt, tights, trunks
FEET: boots, sandals, shoes, socks, trainers
WHOLE BODY: coat, dress, overalls, pyjamas, suit, tracksuit
ACCESSORIES: belt, earrings, gloves, hat, ring, scarf, sunglasses, tie, watch

b.

1. t.shirt
2. tie
3. cap/hat
4. shoes
5. trainers
6. jumper/sweater
7. jacket/suit
8. belt

c. (suggested answers)

warm woollen jacket, a short leather skirt, a thin cotton T-shirt, etc.

d.

1. get undressed, take off
2. got dressed, put on
3. try on, wearing, took off
4. get changed, wear
5. took off, got undressed

e. (open answers)

Communications (pp. 41–42)

a.

LETTERS: envelope, address, postbox, postcode, stamp
TELEPHONE & FAX: dial, message, mobile, phone book, phone number
E-MAIL: e-mail address, keyboard, message, mouse, screen
NEWSPAPERS & MAGAZINES: daily, headlines, journalist, weather forecast
TV & RADIO: channel, journalist, remote control, satellite dish, screen, the 10 o'clock news, weather forecast

b.

2. d. world news
3. b. business news
4. a. sports news
5. c. book review
6. f. feature

c.

1. c
2. d
3. e
4. b
5. a

d.

1. speak, calling, get through, returning, put you through
2. Is that, 'm afraid, be back, leave, give, 's got

Answer key

Computers & the Internet (pp. 43–44)

a.

1. monitor, keyboard
2. laser printer
3. floppy disk
4. laptop

b.

1. c
2. f
3. d
4. h
5. e
6. a.
7. b
8. g

c.

1. hard disk
2. laser printer
3. laptop
4. Internet
5. keyboard
6. online shopping
7. website
8. CD-ROM
9. floppy disk
10. a word processor
11. e-mail
12. a printout
13. network

d. (open answers)

e.

1. after *To:*
2. claire@lanet.co.uk
3. yes, keith@skymail.com
4. yes, new e-mail address
5. happy
6. yes, schooladdresses.doc

Education (pp. 45–46)

a.

1. drawing pin
2. text book
3. scissors
4. rubber
5. pencil
6. ruler
7. timetable

b.

2. desk
3. board
4. notice board

c.

1. Architecture – j
2. Art – d
3. Business Studies – l
4. Chemistry – k
5. Geography – h
6. Information Technology – i
7. History – a
8. Languages – m
9. Maths – f
10. Medicine – b
11. Physical Education – c
12. Physics – e
13. Politics – g

d. (open answers)

e.

1. sports centre
2. student card
3. degree
4. full-time course
5. lecturers
6. term

f.

0. D
1. A
2. C
3. A
4. C
5. D
6. B
7. A
8. C
9. B
10. D

Entertainment (pp. 47–48)

a.

MUSIC: band, classical, composer, concert hall, guitar, musical, musician, opera, orchestra, rock group, pop group, singer, songwriter, violin
ART: artist, exhibition, gallery, painter, sculpture
LITERATURE: novelist, poetry
CINEMA: actor, cartoon, director, film, producer,
THEATRE: actor, director, musical, opera, play, producer, stage

b.

1. c
2. a
3. d
4. e
5. b / c
6. f

c.

1. go to, watch
2. appear
3. listen to
4. see, read
5. played, listen to/see
6. sing
7. played

d.

1. a composer/musician
2. writer/dramatist/playwright
3. film director
4. pop)singer
5. artist/painter
6. actress

e.

1. d
2. e
3. j
4. a
5. h
6. b
7. k
8. g
9. f
10. c

f. (open answers)

Environment (pp. 49–50)

(Note: some of these can be found both in the countryside and in towns)
a. Suggested answers: *Countryside*: bush, cottage, farm, fields, forest, grass, hedge, hills, lake, path, pebble, river, sand, sea, stream, valley, wild flowers, waterfall
Town: bank, car park, library, museum, shops, town hall

b.

1. g
2. e / h
3. f
4. a
5. c
6. d
7. h
8. b

c.

1. The Alps are a mountain range (i)
2. The Mediterranean is a sea (l)
3. Italy is a country (b)
4. The Nile is a river (k)
5. The Atlantic is an ocean (j)
6. Africa is a continent (a)
7. The Bahamas are a group of islands (e)
8. The Sahara is a desert (c)

9. Everest is a mountain (h)
10. The Black Forest is a forest (d)
11. The Amazon is a jungle (f)
12. Cyprus is an island (g)

d.

√: recycled paper, solar panels, bicycles, bottle banks, conservation, ozone layer

✕: acid rain, litter, traffic jam, global warming, factories, sprays, chemicals, exhaust fumes

e.

SHOULD: protect tropical rainforests, plant more trees, recycle paper, protect/save endangered species

SHOULDN'T: waste energy, throw away plastic bags, cut down trees, destroy forests

f.

1. planet		6.	oceans
2. sources of energy		7.	climate
3. global warming		8.	fossil fuels
4. gas		9.	energy
5. storms		10.	poorer countries

Family & relations (pp. 51–52)

a.

1. She is my mother
2. He is my grandfather
3. She is my granddaughter
4. She is my aunt
5. She is my daughter
6. She is my grandmother
7. He is my son
8. He is my father
9. She is my wife
10. He is my uncle
11. She is my sister
12. He is my grandson
13. He is my nephew
14. He is my brother
15. She is my niece

b.

1. first name
2. old friend
3. single parent family
4. have a baby
5. divorced
6. get married
7. get a divorce
8. only child
9. single
10. surname

c.

1. g
2. j
3. i
4. a
5. h
6. c
7. e
8. d
9. f
10. b

d. (open answers)

Food & drink (pp. 53–54)

a.

meat:	bacon, beef, chicken, duck, ham, lamb, pork, sausages, steak
fish:	salmon, sardines
fruit:	apples, bananas, cherry, grapes, lemon, melon, oranges
vegetables:	beetroot, beans, cauliflower, carrot, mushrooms, onions, pepper, potato
dessert:	biscuit, chocolate cake, cream, fruit salad

b.

S	T	O	R	E	T	G	R	A	P	E
P	E	P	P	E	R	A	N	N	I	S
E	L	M	O	T	I	R	U	E	N	T
C	A	U	L	I	F	L	O	W	E	R
A	N	S	T	R	C	I	T	H	A	A
R	O	H	B	E	O	C	H	S	P	W
R	A	R	E	N	O	P	A	N	P	B
O	G	O	I	W	E	E	S	O	L	E
T	R	O	D	A	P	A	D	I	E	R
I	N	M	R	E	S	C	U	F	O	R
M	E	L	O	N	C	H	E	R	R	Y

c.

1. salmon – fish, not meat
2. egg – not milk product
3. peach – fruit, not vegetable
4. pork – not poultry
5. beer – alcoholic

d.

1. some bottles of: beer, coke, milk, olive oil, wine, water
2. a bag of: flour, pears, sweets, tea
3. some cans of: beer, coke, fish, orange juice
4. a carton of: milk, orange juice
5. a jar of: coffee, honey, jam
6. a packet of: chewing gum, coffee, flour, rice, spaghetti, sugar

e. (open answers)

f. (open answers)

Free time, leisure & hobbies (pp. 55–56)

a.

Activities at home: board games, cards, chess, listening to CDs, cooking, DIY, gardening, reading, playing computer games, playing the violin, surfing the Internet, watching videos

Outdoor activities: camping, hiking, hunting, jogging, rock climbing, scuba diving, tennis, window shopping

Things people collect: antiques, coins, stamps

Creative hobbies: cooking, DIY, gardening, painting, photography

b.

1. window shopping
2. cooking
3. playing the violin
4. DIY
5. jogging
6. videos
7. photography / painting

c.

1. d., e.g. clothes, jewels
2. g., e.g. antiques, matchboxes

111

Answer key

3. e., e.g. aerobics, a drawing
4. f., e.g. swimming, camping
5. a., e.g. basketball, the guitar
6. c., e.g. football, videos
7. h., e.g. novels, magazines
8. b., e.g. opera, hard rock

d.

1. – material, needle, pins, scissors
2. – seeds, spade, watering can
3. – olive oil, pasta, saucepan, tomatoes
4. – brush, hammer, nails, paint
5. – balls, net, racket

e. (open answers)

Health & sickness (pp. 57–58)

a.

common problems: a cold, flu, hayfever, a sore throat
aches and pains: a broken wrist, toothache
very serious illnesses: a heart attack, lung cancer, a stroke

b.

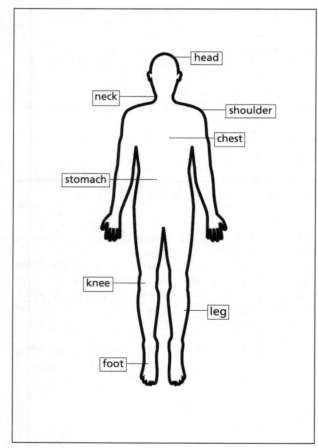

head
neck
shoulder
chest
stomach
knee
leg
foot

c.

1. make an appointment
2. ask questions
3. examine your chest
4. take these pills, write a prescription

5. stay in bed
6. go to the chemist

d.

1. . . . so her tooth would stop hurting
2. . . . to keep you fit
3. . . . should get some fresh air
4. . . . is bad for your heart
5. . . . you've got flu

e. (open answers)

f. (suggested answers)

1. Have you ever burnt your hand?
2. Have you ever been in hospital?
3. Have you ever had an injection?
4. Have you ever been in an ambulance?
5. Have you ever had your eyes tested?

House & home (pp. 59–60)

a.

Sitting Room – armchair, coffee table book, cupboard, sofa, video
Kitchen – cupboard, fridge, kettle, sink
Bedroom – alarm clock, pillow, sheets, wardrobe
Bathroom – bathmat, shower, towels, washbasin

b. (suggested answers)

1. . . . .you sleep
2. . . . . bath. . . shower
3. . . . .. read . . . do your homework
4. . . . sit down . . . relax . . . watch TV
5. . . . the cooking
6. . . . dinner / a meal
7. . . . your tools / laundry
8. . . . you have visitors stay

c. (open answers)

d.

1. dishwasher
2. frying pan
3. chest of drawers
4. pillow

e.

1. sofa
2. curtains
3. cooker
4. kettle
5. armchair
6. cupboard
7. fridge
8. video
9. oven
10. carpet

f.

1. caravan
2. castle
3. block of flats
4. tent
5. bungalow
6. cottage
7. house

g.

1. untidy
2. quiet
3. noisy / convenient
4. dark
5. cramped
6. convenient
7. spacious
8. sunny

Languages, countries & nationalities (pp. 61–62)

a.

COUNTRY	NATIONALITY	LANGUAGE
Italy	Italian	Italian
Brazil	Brazilian	Portuguese
Egypt	Egyptian	Arabic
Poland	Polish	Polish
Greece	Greek	Greek
Russia	Russian	Russian
Wales	Welsh	Welsh
Spain	Spanish	Spanish
Argentina	Argentinian	Spanish
United Kingdom	British	English
Germany	German	*German*
Japan	Japanese	Japanese
Portugal	Portuguese	Portuguese
Israel	Israeli	Hebrew
The Netherlands	Dutch	Dutch
Sweden	Swedish	Swedish
Turkey	Turkish	*Turkish*
Saudi Arabia	Saudi Arabian	Arabic
Australia	Australian	English
Mexico	Mexican	Spanish
France	French	French

b.

Austria Australia Japan Japanese Arabic Italian Saudi Arabia Portuguese Brazilian Chinese Egyptian

c.

1. Iceland – not English
2. Italy – not German
3. Brazil – not Spanish
4. China – not Arabic
5. Scotland – not French

d.

1. Portugal
2. South Korea
3. Egypt
4. Austria
5. Spain
6. Finland
7. Peru
8. Czech Republic
9. Wales
10. Sweden

e.

1. Spanish
2. India
3. China
4. India
5. Argentina

6. Hebrew
7. United Kingdom, Australia, Canada, New Zealand, United States of America
8. Egyptian
9. Italy
10. Russian

Money & numbers (pp. 63–64)

a.

1. i
2. e
3. f
4. g
5. h
6. b
7. a
8. j
9. c
10. d

b.

1. won
2. bought, spent
3. gave
4. wasted
5. earns
6. cost, pay
7. borrowed
8. save

c.

1. f
2. h
3. a
4. g
5. c
6. d
7. b
8. e

d. (various answers are acceptable – discuss)

e.

1. How much did this car cost?
2. I earn about £32,000 a year
3. We are going to rent their flat
4. Could I borrow your dictionary?
5. I cannot afford this trip
6. It's a waste of money

f.

0. B
1. B
2. C
3. A
4. D
5. B
6. D
7. B
8. C
9. B
10. C

Opinions & feelings (pp. 65–66)

a.

1. loves, likes
2. hates, doesn't like
3. don't mind
4. love
5. hates, doesn't like

b.

1. **I love**, I really like, I feel very happy about
2. **I like**, I'm looking forward to, I'm keen on
3. **I don't mind**, It makes no difference to me, I'm bored of
4. **I don't like**, I don't enjoy, I sometimes worry about
5. **I hate**, I loathe, I really dislike

c. (open answers)

113

Answer key

d.

1. . . . feels . . .
2. . . . thinks (that) . . .
3. . . . persuade . . .
4. . . . refuses . . .
5. . . . enjoys . . .
6. . . . suggests . . .
7. . . . recommends . . .
8. . . . offers . . .
9. . . . keen on . . .
10. . . . disappointed . . .

e.

AGREEING: I quite agree / Yes, that's true / I think you're right
DISAGREEING: I totally disagree / Maybe, but don't forget / I don't think so / You could be right, but
GIVING OPINION: In my opinion / I think / Personally / According to / As far as I am concerned

f.

1. . . . opinion you
2. . . . I think you're
3. . . . to the newspaper
4. . . . as I am concerned
5. . . . totally disagree with you

People & descriptions (pp. 67–68)

a.

GENERAL: beautiful, good-looking, handsome, pretty, plain
FACE AND HEAD: bald, a beard, blonde, curly, fair, a fringe, green eyes, light brown, long, pale skin, a ponytail, a pointed nose, straight
HEIGHT AND BUILD: fat, medium height, petite, short, skinny, slim, tall, thin
AGE: elderly, in his early thirties, middle-aged, in his teens, young

b. (suggested answers)

1. hair
2. tall
3. hair, eyes
4. looking, young
5. hair, skin
6. ponytail

c. (open answers)

d. (suggested answers)

POSITIVE: cheerful, clever, flexible, generous, kind, relaxed, reliable, strong
NEGATIVE: aggressive, cruel, dishonest, lazy, mean, miserable, pessimistic, stubborn, stupid, tense, unfriendly, weak

e.

1. d
2. c
3. f
4. g
5. b
6. e
7. h
8. a

f.

BOX A: blonde – fair, bright – clever, fat – overweight, good-looking – handsome, nervous – tense, cheerful – optimistic, easy-going – relaxed
BOX B: attractive – plain, careful – careless, cheerful – miserable, hard-working – lazy, foolish – wise, strong – weak, confident – shy

g. (open answers)

Places & buildings pp.69–70

a. (suggested answers)

1. c. language school
2. b. hotel room
3. e. a restaurant
4. f. seaside resort
5. d. an office
6. g. small town
7. a. health club

b.

1. library
2. museum
3. bank
4. town hall
5. post office
6. pedestrian zone
7. square
8. theatre

c.

ART GALLERY: artist, drawing, exhibition, painting, sculpture
WILDLIFE PARK: elephant, fence, giraffe, lions, monkeys
MARKET: antiques, arcade, bargains, clothes, fruit, old CDs, souvenirs, stall, vegetables

d.

1. skyscraper
2. basement
3. garage
4. pavement
5. bungalow
6. letterbox
7. front door
8. balcony
9. attic
10. gate

e.

1. c
2. f
3. i
4. g
5. h
6. d
7. a
8. e
9. b

Restaurants & cooking (pp. 71–72)

a.

1. book
2. courses
3. starter
4. main
5. dessert
6. aperitif
7. rare
8. well-done
9. bill
10. tip

b.

1. Three
2. Smoked salmon pâté served with hot toast'
3. the steak
4. 'Pork fillet in white wine'
5. 'Double chocolate ice cream'
6. 'Baked apple and coconut pudding'
7. 'Prawn and cucumber salad'
8. No, because it has a spicy sauce
9. £57
10. No

c.

1. order, made, served
2. bring
3. show, take
4. serves, have, book

d.

boil / in water above the heat e.g. carrots, spaghetti
bake / in the oven without oil e.g. cakes, bread
grill / under the heat e.g. toast, steak
fry / in oil or butter above the heat e.g. chips, sausages
roast / in the oven using oil e.g. meat, potatoes

e. (open answers)

f. (suggested answers)

1.	pepper	5.	coffee
2.	garlic	6.	steak
3.	butter	7.	wine
4.	onions		

Shopping (pp. 73–75)

a.

1.	d	6.	i
2.	e	7.	a
3.	f	8.	c
4.	g	9.	b
5.	h		

b.

CLOTHES: boots, a jacket, a jumper, a suit
FURNITURE: a bookcase, a sofa
ELECTRICAL APPLIANCES: a dishwasher, a freezer, a lamp
HOUSEHOLD GOODS: coffee, kitchen roll, salt, shampoo, sugar, washing powder
STATIONERY: envelopes, a file, a notebook, pens, postcards, writing paper
FRUIT: apples, bananas, melon, oranges, peaches

c.

2.	window shopping	5.	shopping centre
3.	shopping list	6.	shoplifter
4.	shop window	7.	shopping bag

d.

1.	B	3.	D
2.	C	4.	A

e.

1. Yes, here you are.
2. All right, £25 then.
3. They're £5 each. Crystal.
4. The oval ones, I think.
5. Hello, can I help you?
6. No, that's too big. Do you have anything smaller?
7. What a pity! Thanks anyway.

f. (open answers)

Signs & notices (pp. 76–78)

a.

1.	instruction	7.	instruction
2.	information	8.	instruction
3.	instruction	9.	information
4.	instruction	10.	instruction
5.	information	11.	instruction
6.	instruction	12.	information

b. (suggested answers)

1. restaurant, library, airport
2. public phone
3. street
4. airport
5. restaurant, cinema
6. library
7. public park
8. bus
9. hotel room door, post-it on someone's desk
10. cinema
11. hotel reception
12. clothes shop

c.

1.	use, instructions	7.	area, card
2.	no longer, hour	8.	seat, disabled
3.	put	9.	Changing rooms, may
4.	forbidden, allowed	10.	on time, cancelled
5.	entrance	11.	responsible, property
6.	Passengers, luggage	12.	warning

d.

a. . . . mustn't walk . . .
b. . . . may have breakfast . . .
c. . . . mustn't keep . . .
d. . . . should drive . . .
e. . . . must have your . . .
f. . . . should queue here . . .
g. . . . may use . . .
h. . . . mustn't dive in . . .

e. (open answers)

Sport (pp. 79–80)

a.

1.	basketball	6.	ice skating
2.	golf	7.	rubgy
3.	tennis	8.	skiing
4.	football	9.	athletics
5.	baseball	10.	swimming

b.

baseball, basketball, cricket, football, golf, hockey, rugby, table tennis, tennis

c. (suggested answers)

athletics, climbing, cycling, golf, ice skating, skiing, swimming

d. (open answers)

e.

Name of sport: baseball, boxing, car racing, swimming
Place: court, field, pitch, pool, slope, stadium, track
Equipment: ball, basket, crash helmet, gloves, golf clubs, net, racket, shorts, skis, trunks, whistle

f.

1.	c	4.	e
2.	f	5.	d
3.	a	6.	b

Answer key

g.

1. do, go
2. play, do
3. go, playing
4. plays, do, go

h. (open answers)

i.

1. c
2. d
3. b
4. d
5. a
6. c
7. b

Transport & travel (pp. 81–82)

a.

BUS: bus stop, coach, crossroads, driver, junction, station
AIR: airport, flight attendant, helicopter, pilot, runway, terminal
TRAIN: carriage, driver, platform, railway, station
CAR: cab, crossroads, driver, junction, motorway, taxi, traffic lights
SEA: ferry, harbour

b.

1. d
2. e
3. a
4. f
5. c
6. b

c.

1. slow
2. uncomfortable
3. crowded
4. expensive
5. cheap

d.

DEPARTURES: air terminal, boarding card, check-in desk, duty-free, departure lounge, excess baggage
THE FLIGHT: cabin crew, pilot, runway, seat belt, take-off, upright position
ARRIVALS: air terminal, customs, landing

e.

1. excess baggage
2. cabin crew
3. air terminal
4. check-in desk
5. upright position

f.

0. C
1. B
2. C
3. A
4. D
5. B
6. D
7. D
8. C
9. A
10. B

Weather (pp. 83–84)

a.

1. sun – sunny
2. ice – icy
3. fog – foggy
4. mist – misty
5. climate-climatic
6. shower – showery
7. humidity – humid
8. cloud – cloudy
9. wind – windy
10. heat – hot

b.

1. cloudy
2. sunny
3. windy
4. snow
5. below zero
6. thunderstorms
7. rain

c.

1. False – A shower is a light rain.
2. False – It never pours with rain in the desert.
3. True
4. False – It rarely gets frosty . . .
5. True
6. False – If it is humid the air will be wet.
7. True
8. False – Lightning is a flash of electricity in the sky followed by thunder.
9. True
10. False – temperatures below zero are very usual in the mountains in Switzerland

d.

1. h
2. d
3. e
4. a
5. f
6. b
7. g
8. c

e.

1. C
2. B
3. C
4. A
5. B
6. C
7. B
8. A
9. A
10. B

f.

A. hot and dry, below –20ºC, snow, little rain
B. tropical, 24 and 27ºC, wet season, very humid
C. hot and dry, fresh breeze, sunshine, not too cold

g. (open answers)

Work & jobs (pp. 85–87)

a.

EDUCATION: lecturer, professor, teacher, tutor
HEALTH: dentist, doctor, nurse, psychologist, surgeon
PUBLIC SERVICES: dustman, firefighter, police officer, social worker, taxi driver, traffic warden
MANUAL JOBS: builder, plumber
MEDIA: editor, journalist, newscaster, publisher, reporter, writer

b.

1. c
2. f
3. h
4. k
5. i
6. j
7. g
8. l
9. b
10. a
11. e
12. d

c.

JOB	PLACE	DUTIES
pilot	*aeroplane*	*flies a plane*
librarian	library	works in a library
reporter	*newspaper*	writes newspaper reports
secretary	*office*	*writes letters, answers the phone, files documents for someone*
vet	veterinary surgery hospital	looks after sick animals
History teacher	*school*	teaches History
lecturer	university	gives lectures to students
plumber	*people's homes*	fixes water pipes
hairdresser	*the hairdresser's*	*cuts people's hair*
police officer	police station	*Enforces the law*

d.

Right order: 5, 1, 8, 7, 4, 2, 3, 6

e.

1.	f	5.	a
2.	h	6.	d
3.	g	7.	c
4.	e	8.	b

f.

1.	in charge of	4.	salary is
2	involves visiting	5.	nine-to-five
3.	an early retirement	6.	income is

g. (open answers)

Phonetic symbols (pp. 88–89)

a.

1. /bæk/ /ˈbeiˈkʼn/
2. /kɒf/ /ˈɪˈnʌf/
3. /vɑz/ /ˈreɪ·zər/
4. /ˈkʌrɪ/ /ˈkɜːtn/
5. /naʊ/ /nɜʊ/
6. /θruː/ /θrɜʊ/

b.

1.	f	6.	j
2.	e	7.	d
3.	h	8.	a
4.	I	9.	b
5.	g	10.	c

c.

1.	/ˈɑrɪndʒ	6.	/greɪ/
2.	/waɪt/	7.	/pɪŋk/
3	/beɪʒ/	8.	/ˈpɜːpl/
4	/ˈjelɜʊ/	9.	/griːn/
5.	/braʊn/	10.	/bluː/

d.

1.	s	5.	w
2.	k	6.	k
3.	w	7.	h
4.	h		

e.

1.	beard	13.	mould
2.	bead	14.	peace
3.	threat	15.	said
4.	fear	16.	foul
5.	beak	17.	wool
6.	horse	18.	gone
7.	height	19.	watch
8.	home	20.	choose
9.	wound	21.	wander
10.	few	22.	work
11.	town	23.	foot
12.	bear	24.	vase

Punctuation & spelling (pp. 90–91)

a.

1.	d. VIII	7.	j. II
2.	f. XI	8.	a. V
3.	i. IV	9.	e. I
4.	k. VI	10.	c. VII
5.	g. X	11.	h. III
6.	b. IX		

b.

1. What an amazing story!
2. I ran all the way to the station, but I still missed the train.
3. 'Come and see what's happened', said John.
4. I spoke to David yesterday; he can't come to the meeting tonight.
5. 'What's your passport number?', the policeman asked.
6. 'I need some butter, eggs, yoghurt and sugar.
7. 'I don't know who's ordered this, but it wasn't me', the old man said.
8. The car (the one with broken window) was parked outside our house.

c.

1.	basketball	6.	golf
2.	boxing	7.	rugby
3.	cricket	8.	skiing
4.	cycling	9.	swimming
5.	football	10.	tennis

d.

1.	weight	5.	which
2.	whale	6.	white
3.	wheat	7.	why
4.	wheel	8.	wild

e. (spoken answers)

f.

1.	houses	4.	losses
2.	matches	5.	babies
3.	faxes	6.	universities

117

Answer key

g.

1.	dear	6.	tale
2.	brake	7.	great
3.	sale	8.	waist
4.	flour	9.	sew
5.	quiet	10.	mail

Word stress & pronunciation (pp. 92–93)

a.

grateful, happy, jealous, miserable, thoughtful, worried

b.

1.	father	9.	computer
2.	education	10.	photographer
3.	necessary	11.	anxious
4.	fortunately	12.	below
5.	advertisement	13.	preferred
6.	organise	14.	expected
7.	dangerous	15.	police
8.	wonderful		

c.

1.	record	6.	increase
2.	increase	7.	present
3.	conduct	8.	record
4.	permit	9.	permit
5.	present	10.	conduct

d.

1.	no	6.	no
2.	yes	7.	no
3.	no	8.	yes
4.	yes	9.	yes
5.	no	10.	yes